make me

cupcakes

MURDOCH BOOKS

Contents

Introduction 4

Teatime 6

Just for kids 30

Decorate it 60

Decadent 86

Basics 114

Index 124

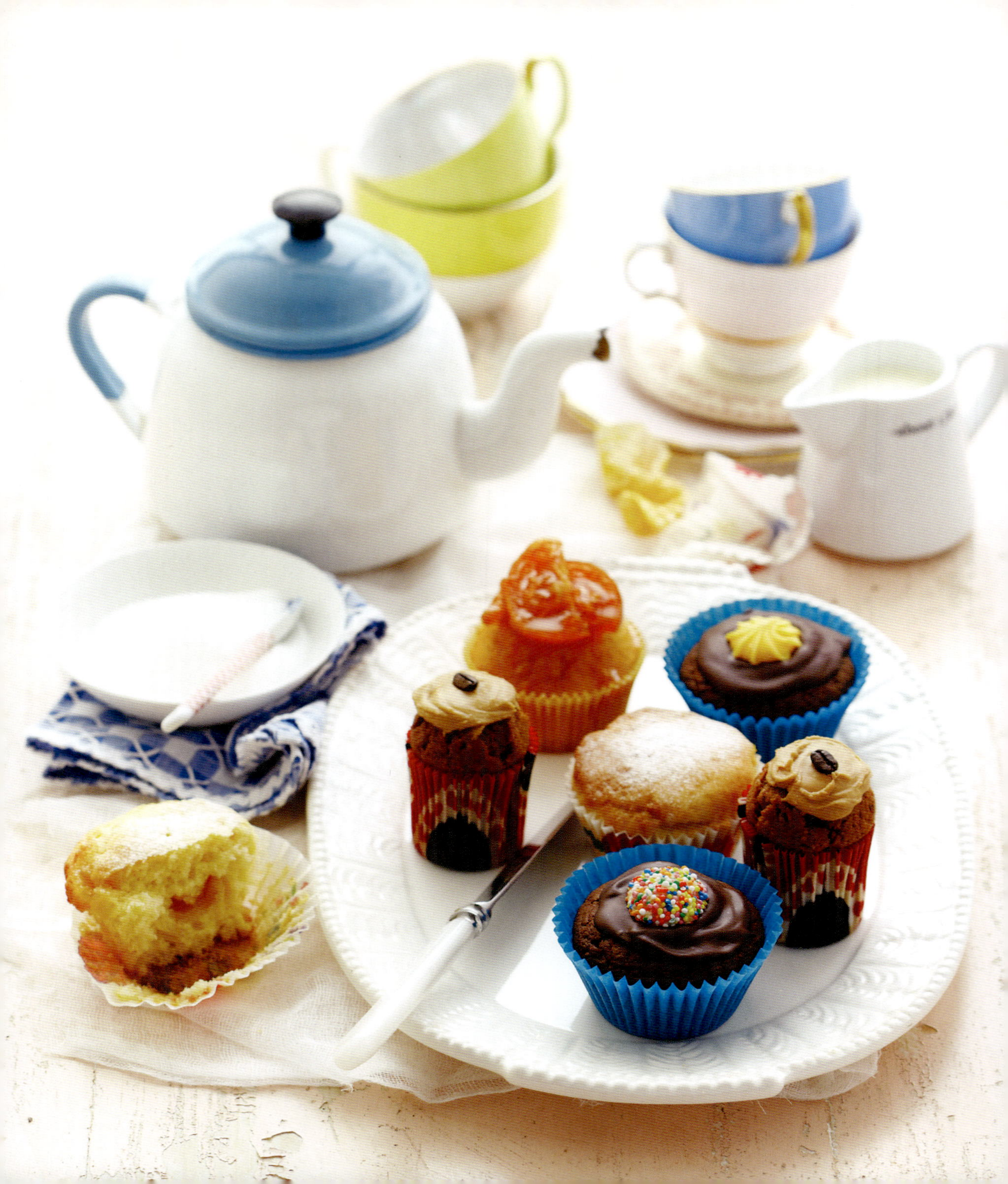

Introduction

Never failing to bring a smile to your face, cupcakes are a perennial favourite with kids and grown-ups alike.

Make Me Cupcakes is packed with 56 inspiring recipes for any occasion. You'll never think of cupcakes the same way again once you've perused the selection of flavours and decorating ideas: from lime delicious to balsamic raspberry, from classic caramel and walnut to tangy lemon meringue and from hungry caterpillars to cuddly baby bears.

At the back of this book you'll find a comprehensive basics section covering everything from basic cupcakes including vanilla, chocolate and gluten free – in all different sizes – to an array of icings. These never-fail recipes will allow you to mix and match and develop your own eye-catching creations.

You'll be charmed by these handheld delights. Whatever the occasion, make it special with cupcakes.

Teatime

Apricot, sour cream & coconut cupcakes

Preparation time: 20 minutes
Cooking time: 25 minutes
Makes: 20 standard cupcakes

125 g (4½ oz) unsalted butter
220 g (7¾ oz/1 cup) caster sugar
260 g (9¼ oz/1¾ cups) self-raising flour
45 g (1¾ oz/½ cup) desiccated coconut
2 eggs, at room temperature, lightly beaten
250 ml (9 fl oz/1 cup) apricot nectar
125 g (4½ oz/½ cup) sour cream
825 g (1 lb 13 oz) tinned apricot halves in juice, drained (you need 20 apricot halves)
115 g (4 oz/⅓ cup) warmed, sieved apricot jam

TIP: Keep cupcakes brushed with jam in an airtight container in the fridge for up to 1 day.

1 Preheat oven to 180°C (350°F/Gas 4). Line 20 standard (80 ml/2½ fl oz/⅓ cup) muffin holes with paper cases.
2 Melt the butter and sugar in a small saucepan over low heat, stirring until the sugar dissolves. Remove from the heat and set aside to cool slightly. Sift the flour into a large mixing bowl, add the coconut and make a well in the centre. Put the egg, apricot nectar and sour cream in a medium bowl and whisk to combine. Add both the butter and egg mixtures to the well in the dry ingredients and stir with a wooden spoon until combined.
3 Divide the mixture evenly among the paper cases and place an apricot half, cut side down, on the top of each cupcake.
4 Bake for 20 minutes or until a skewer comes out clean when inserted into the centre of a cupcake. Allow to cool for 5 minutes in the tins before transferring to a wire rack to cool completely.
5 Meanwhile, heat the jam in a small saucepan over low heat until melted. Brush a little jam over each cooled cupcake.

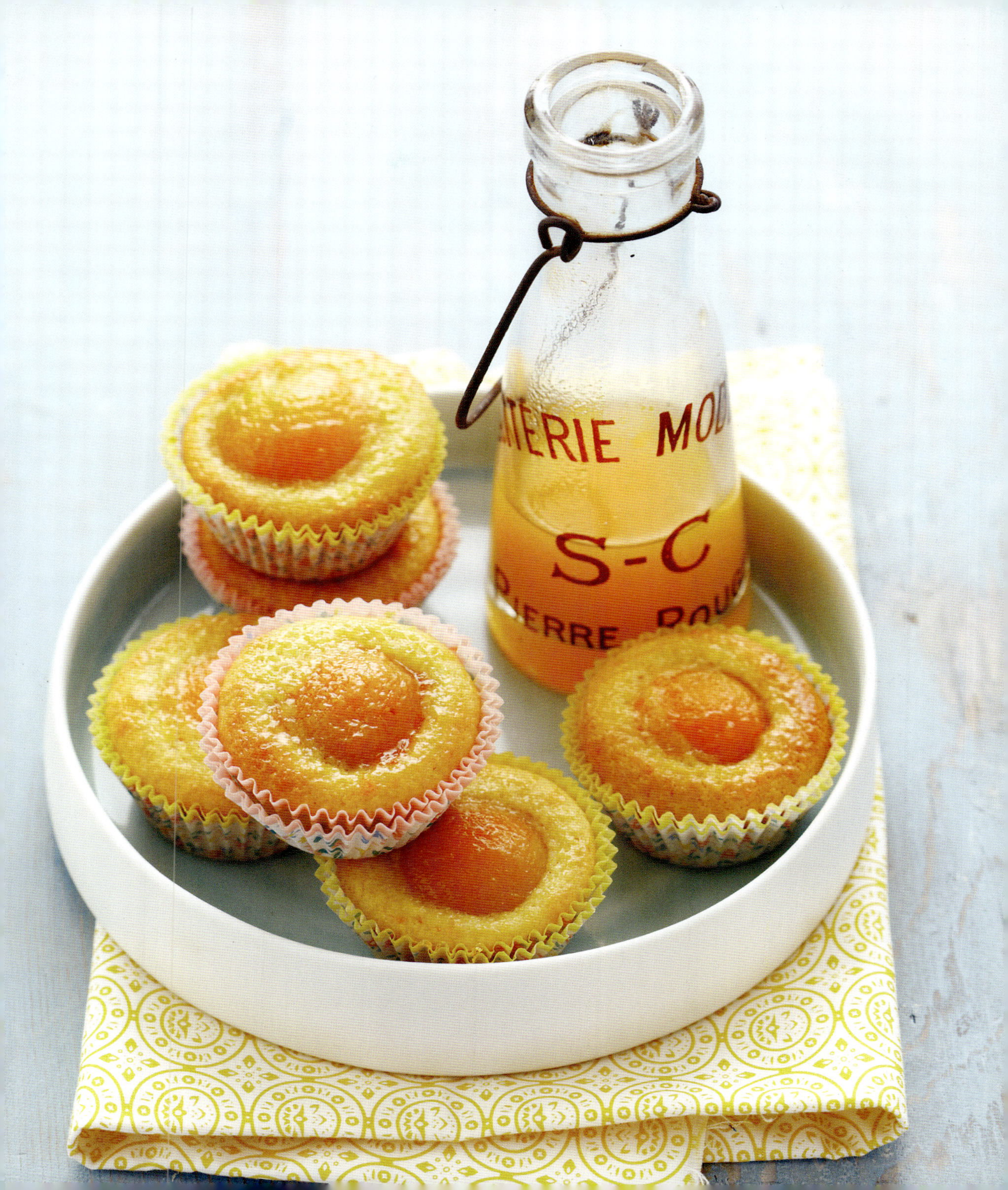
TERIE MOD
S-C
IERRE ROU

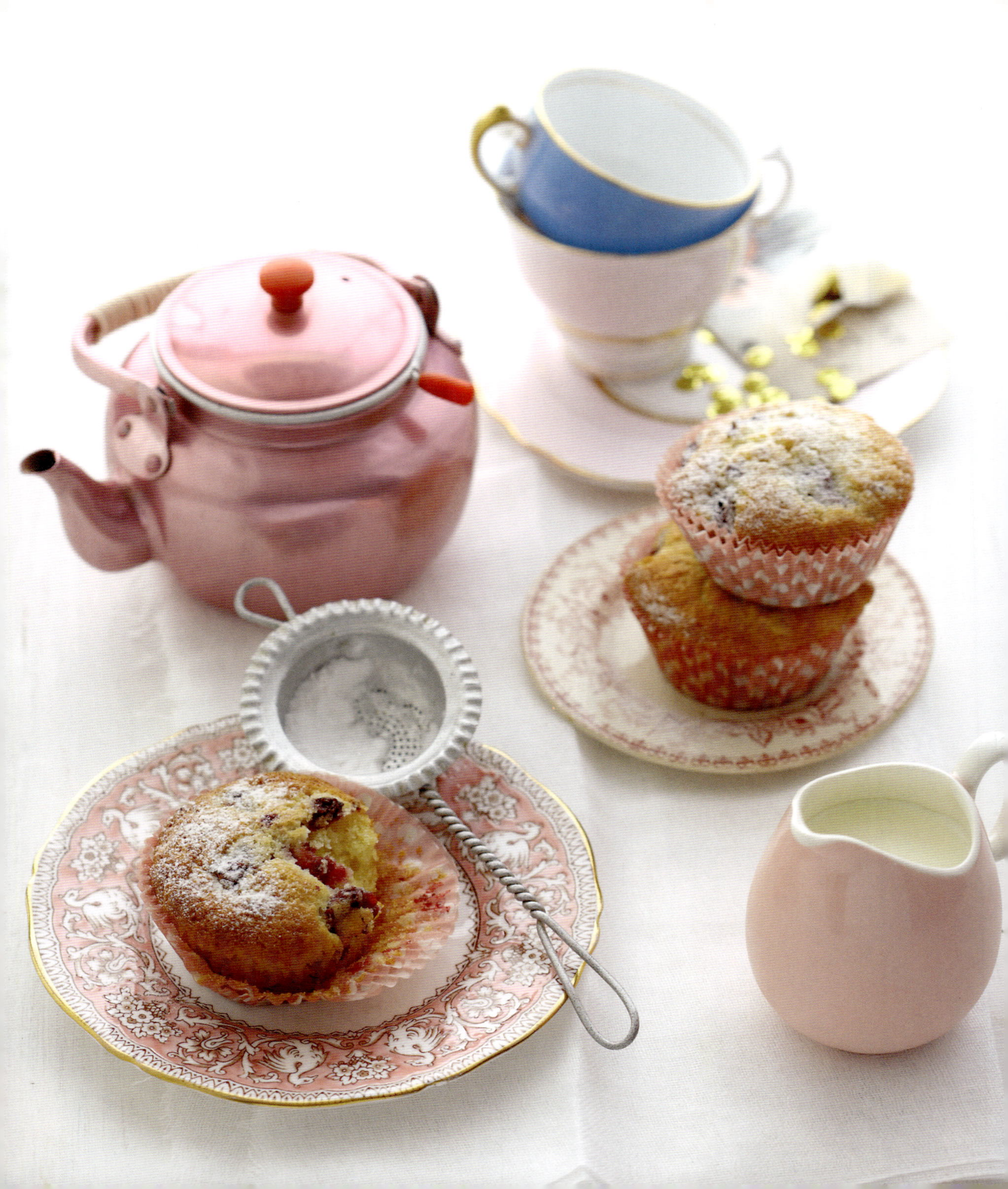

Cherry cupcakes

Preparation time: 15 minutes
Cooking time: 20 minutes
Makes: 12 standard cupcakes

125 g (4½ oz) unsalted butter, softened
165 g (5¾ oz/¾ cup) caster sugar
2 eggs, at room temperature
225 g (8 oz/1½ cups) self-raising flour, sifted
125 ml (4 fl oz/½ cup) milk
250 g (9 oz/1¼ cups) well-drained, pitted, bottled morello cherries, halved
pure icing sugar, to dust

1 Preheat oven to 180°C (350°F/Gas 4). Line 12 standard (80 ml/2½ fl oz/⅓ cup) muffin holes with paper cases.
2 Use an electric mixer to beat the butter and sugar together in a medium bowl until pale and creamy. Add the eggs, one at a time, beating well after each addition. Use a large metal spoon or spatula to fold in the flour and milk alternately in two separate batches each. Gently fold in the cherries. Divide the mixture evenly among the paper cases.
3 Bake for 18–20 minutes or until a skewer inserted into the centre of a cupcake comes out clean. Allow to cool for 5 minutes in the tin before transferring to a wire rack to cool completely.
4 Serve dusted with the icing sugar.

TIP: These cupcakes are best served on the day of making.

Lamington cupcakes

Preparation time: 10 minutes
Cooking time: nil
Decorating time: 40 minutes
Makes: 12 standard cupcakes

12 standard vanilla cupcakes (see page 116), cooked without paper cases
1 quantity chocolate glacé icing (see page 121)
130 g (4½ oz/2 cups) shredded coconut
250 ml (9 fl oz/1 cup) thickened (whipping) cream
1 teaspoon pure icing sugar, sifted

1 Place a wire rack over a baking tray or sheet of baking paper. Cut the top third off each of the cupcakes.
2 Put the glacé icing in a medium bowl (you may need to stir in a little water to achieve a dipping consistency). Put the coconut in a small shallow bowl. Use a fork to dip the top and base cupcake pieces into the icing, turning to coat all but the cut surfaces. Place cut side down on the wire rack. Stand for 2–3 minutes or until the icing is almost set. Dip each cupcake piece in the coconut, turning to coat the icing. Return the cupcakes to the wire rack. Stand for 10–15 minutes or until the icing is completely set.
3 Put the cream and icing sugar in a medium bowl and use electric beaters with a whisk attachment to whisk until firm peaks form. Use a piping bag fitted with a 1 cm (½ in) plain nozzle to pipe the cream onto the cut side of each cupcake base. Top with the remaining cupcake pieces cut side down.

> **TIPS:** Use a fork to remove the cupcake halves from the glacé icing to allow any excess icing to drizzle off.
>
> Drain the cupcakes cut side down on the wire rack so that the icing evenly coats them.
>
> Keep uniced cupcakes in an airtight container in the fridge for up to 2 days.

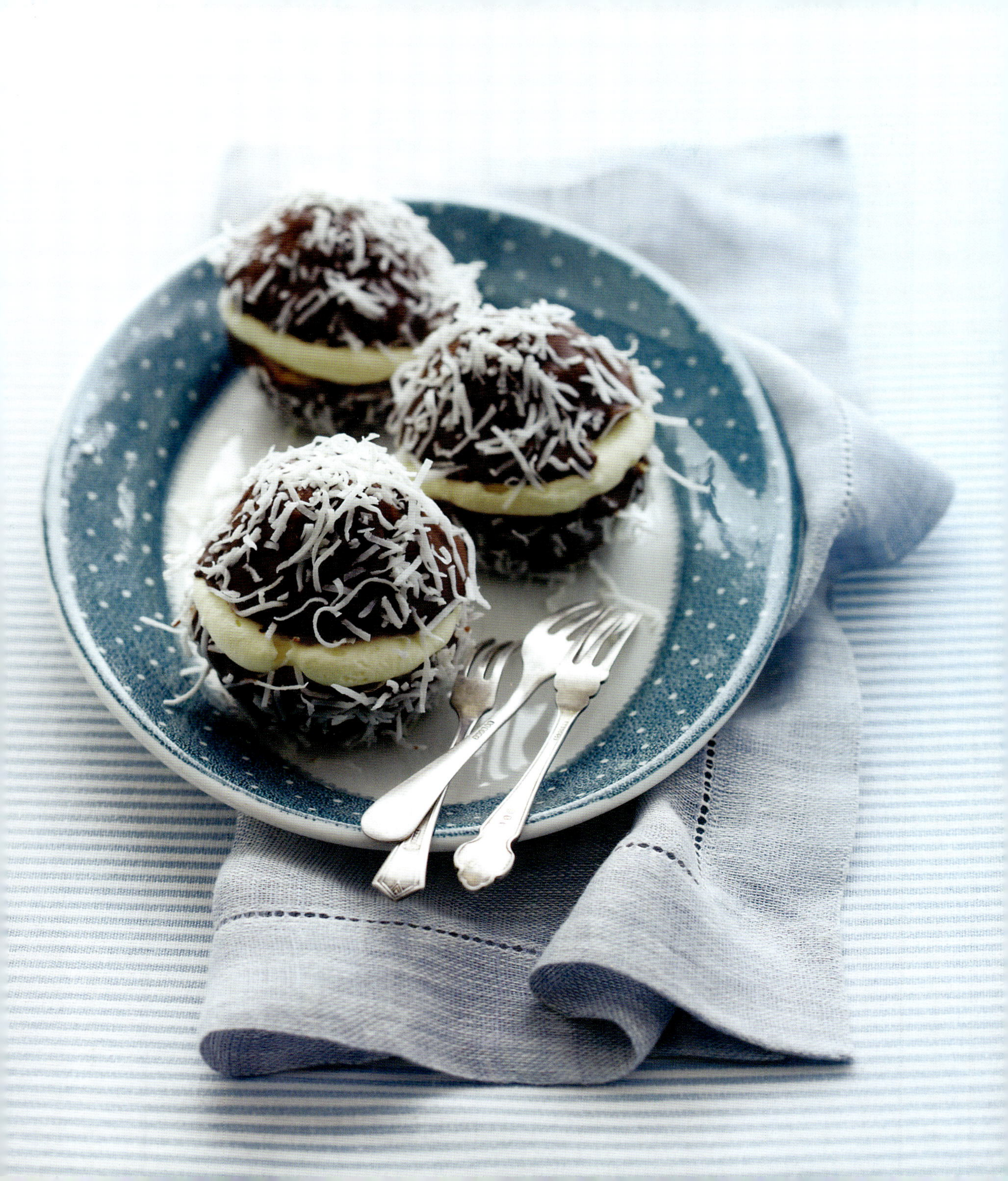

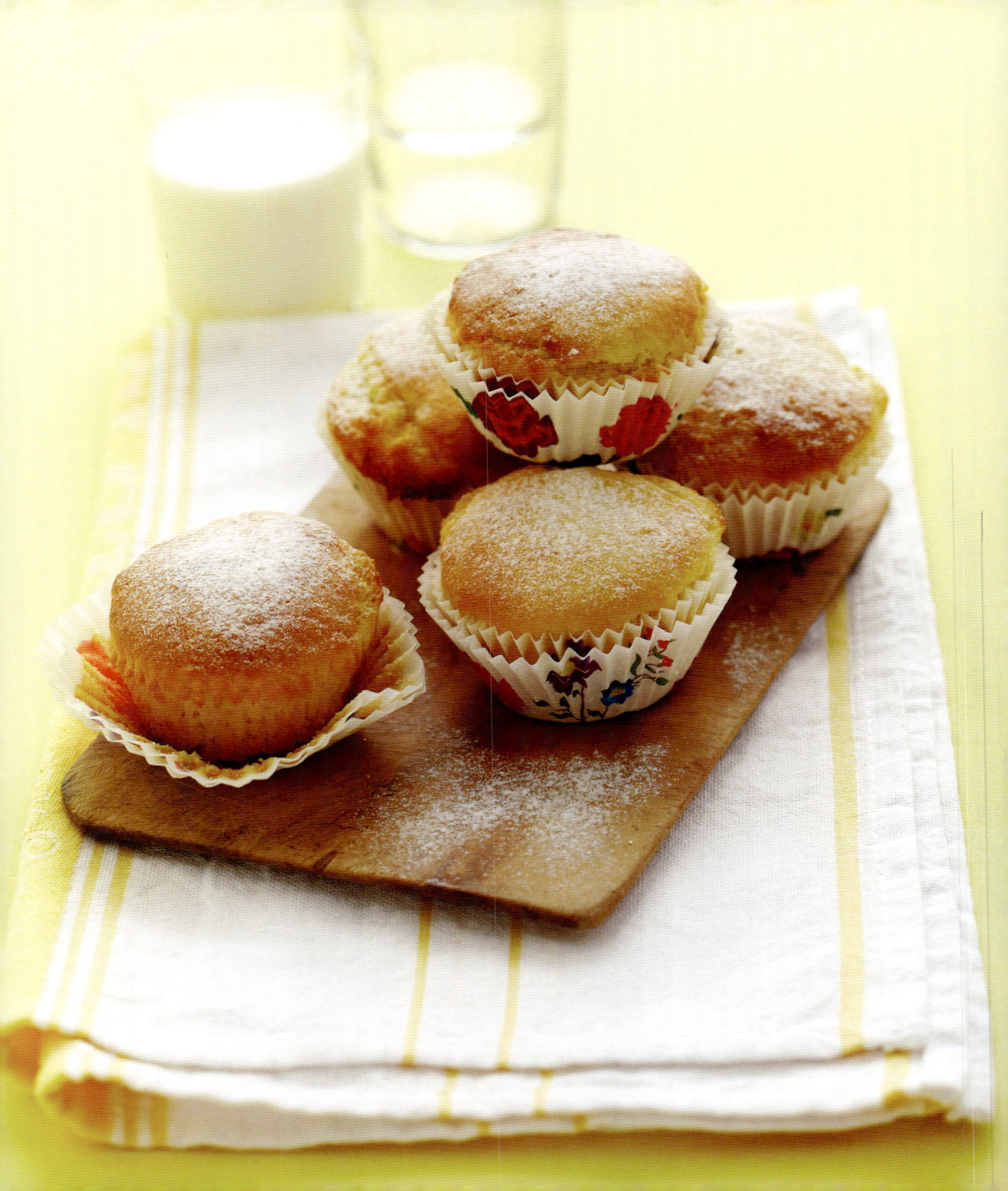

Little marmalade cakes

Preparation time: 20 minutes
Cooking time: 20 minutes
Makes: 12 standard cupcakes

335 g (11¾ oz/2¼ cups) self-raising flour, sifted
165 g (5¾ oz/¾ cup) caster sugar
250 ml (9 fl oz/1 cup) milk
2 eggs, at room temperature, lightly beaten
½ teaspoon vanilla extract
75 g (2¾ oz) unsalted butter, melted
115 g (4 oz/⅓ cup) orange marmalade (see tip)
pure icing sugar, to dust

> **TIPS:** You can use other flavours of marmalade or jam.
>
> These cupcakes are best served on the day of making.

1 Preheat oven to 180°C (350°F/Gas 4). Line 12 standard (80 ml/2½ fl oz/⅓ cup) muffin holes with paper cases.
2 Combine the flour and sugar in a large bowl and make a well in the centre. Put the milk, egg, vanilla and butter in a medium bowl and whisk to combine. Pour the milk mixture into the well in the dry ingredients and use a metal spoon to gradually fold in the milk mixture until just combined. Divide three-quarters of the mixture evenly among the paper cases. Top each with 1 teaspoon of the marmalade and cover with the remaining cake mixture.
3 Bake for 20 minutes or until light golden and the top springs back when gently pressed. Allow to cool for 5 minutes in the tin before transferring to a wire rack to cool completely.
4 Serve dusted with the icing sugar.

Mini fluffy coconut cupcakes

Preparation time: 20 minutes
Cooking time: 12 minutes
Decorating time: 30 minutes
Makes: 48 mini cupcakes

>300 g (10½ oz/2 cups) self-raising flour, sifted
>45 g (1¾ oz/½ cup) desiccated coconut
>220 g (7¾ oz/1 cup) caster sugar
>250 ml (9 fl oz/1 cup) buttermilk
>2 eggs, at room temperature, lightly beaten
>1 teaspoon coconut extract
>125 g (4½ oz) unsalted butter, melted, cooled
>1 quantity vanilla buttercream (see page 123)
>30 g (1 oz/½ cup) flaked coconut, to sprinkle

1 Preheat oven to 180°C (350°F/Gas 4). Line 48 mini (20 ml/½ fl oz /1 tablespoon) muffin holes with paper cases.
2 Combine the flour, desiccated coconut and sugar in a large bowl and make a well in the centre. In a medium bowl combine the buttermilk, egg, coconut extract and butter. Pour the buttermilk mixture into the well in the dry ingredients and mix with a balloon whisk until just combined. Divide the mixture evenly among the paper cases.
3 Bake for 12 minutes or until a skewer inserted into the centre of a cupcake comes out clean. Allow to cool for 5 minutes in the tins before transferring to a wire rack to cool completely.
4 To decorate, spread each cooled cupcake with the buttercream. Put the flaked coconut in a bowl and gently press the top of each cupcake into the coconut.

TIP: Keep iced and decorated cupcakes in an airtight container in the fridge for up to 2 days. Serve at room temperature.

Oatmeal & raspberry cupcakes

Preparation time: 15 minutes
Cooking time: 25 minutes
Makes: 12 standard cupcakes

melted butter, to grease
125 g (4½ oz/1 cup) oatmeal
375 ml (13 fl oz/1½ cups) milk
300 g (10½ oz/2 cups) plain flour
1 tablespoon baking powder
110 g (3¾ oz/½ cup, firmly packed) soft brown sugar
1 egg, at room temperature, lightly beaten
90 g (3¼ oz/¼ cup) honey
60 g (2¼ oz) unsalted butter, melted
155 g (5½ oz/1¼ cups) fresh or frozen (unthawed) raspberries

1 Preheat oven to 190°C (375°F/Gas 5). Grease 12 standard (80 ml/2½ fl oz/⅓ cup) muffin holes.
2 Put the oatmeal in a medium bowl, stir in the milk and set aside for 5 minutes. Sift the flour and baking powder into a large bowl, stir in the sugar and make a well in the centre.
3 Combine the egg, honey and butter in a small bowl and stir to mix well. Pour the egg mixture and oatmeal mixture into the well in the dry ingredients, then use a metal spoon to stir until just combined. Do not overmix – the mixture will still be slightly lumpy. Gently fold in the raspberries. Divide the mixture evenly among the muffin holes.
4 Bake for 20–25 minutes or until golden and a skewer inserted into the centre of a cupcake comes out clean. Allow to cool for 5 minutes in the tin before transferring to a wire rack. Serve warm.

> **TIPS:** Do not overmix the batter or the cupcakes will be heavy.
>
> Keep cupcakes in an airtight container in the fridge for up to 2 days. Serve at room temperature.

Almond & apple cupcakes

Preparation time: 15 minutes
Cooking time: 20 minutes
Makes: 12 standard cupcakes

    175 g (6 oz) unsalted butter, chopped
    100 g (3½ oz/1 cup) almond meal
    210 g (7½ oz/1⅔ cups) pure icing sugar, sifted
    75 g (2¾ oz/½ cup) plain flour, sifted
    5 egg whites, at room temperature
    1 pink lady apple (or apple of your choice)
    1 tablespoon granulated sugar
    1–2 teaspoons cinnamon sugar

1 Preheat oven to 200°C (400°F/Gas 6). Line 12 standard (80 ml/2½ fl oz/⅓ cup) muffin holes with paper cases.
2 Heat the butter in a small saucepan over low heat until melted.
3 Put the almond meal, icing sugar and flour in a large bowl and mix with a wooden spoon to combine. Add the egg whites and use a balloon whisk to combine. Add the cooled melted butter and whisk to combine.
4 Divide the mixture evenly among the paper cases. Dice the apple and sprinkle over the top of the cupcake mixture. Sprinkle with the sugar.
5 Bake for 18–20 minutes, turning the tin around after 12 minutes, or until golden and a skewer inserted into the centre of a cupcake comes out clean. Allow to cool for 5 minutes in the tin then remove and sprinkle with the cinnamon sugar. Serve immediately or transfer to a wire rack to cool completely.

> **TIPS:** These cupcakes are delicious served warm with whipped or thick (double/heavy) cream.
>
> Keep cupcakes in an airtight container in the fridge for up to 2-3 days. Serve at room temperature.

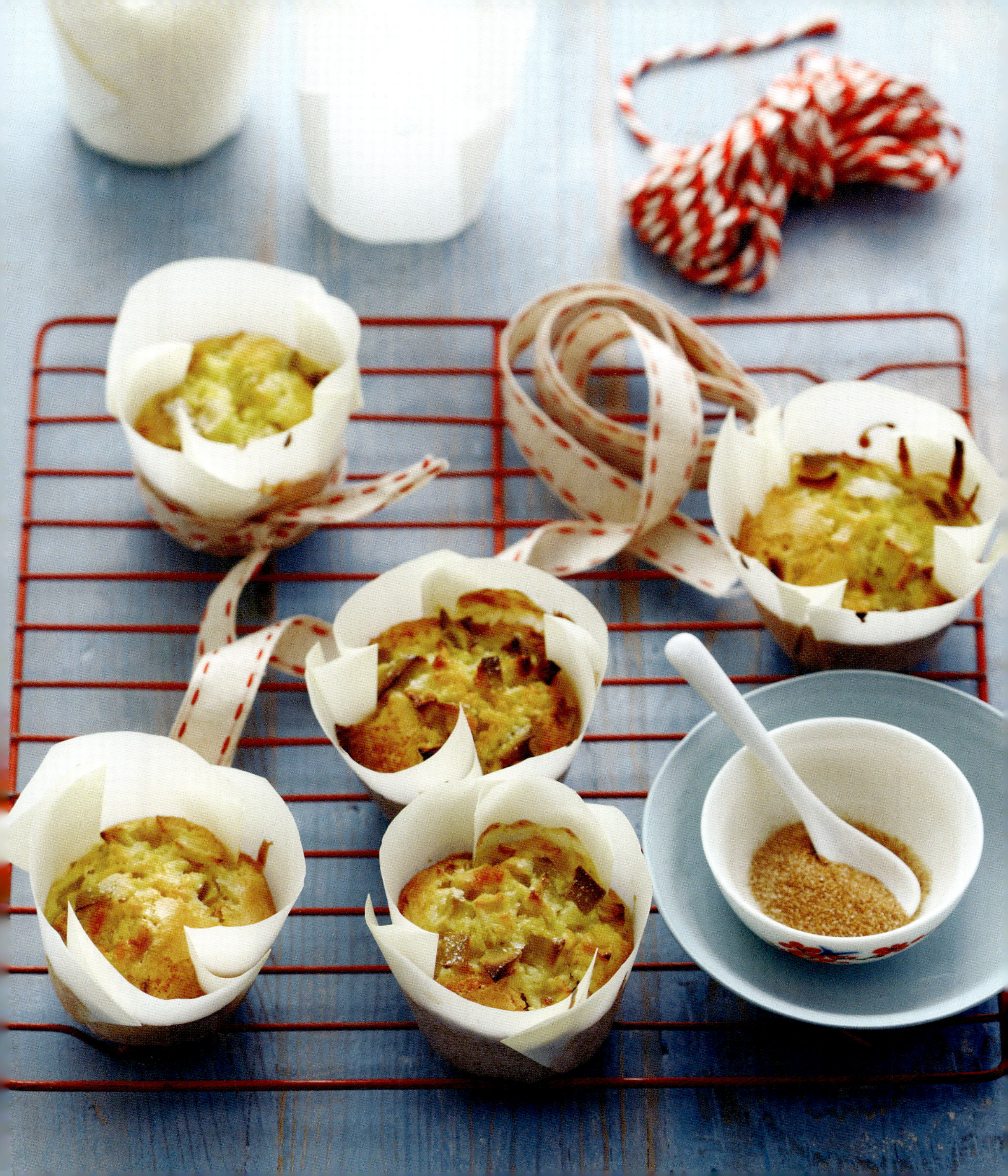

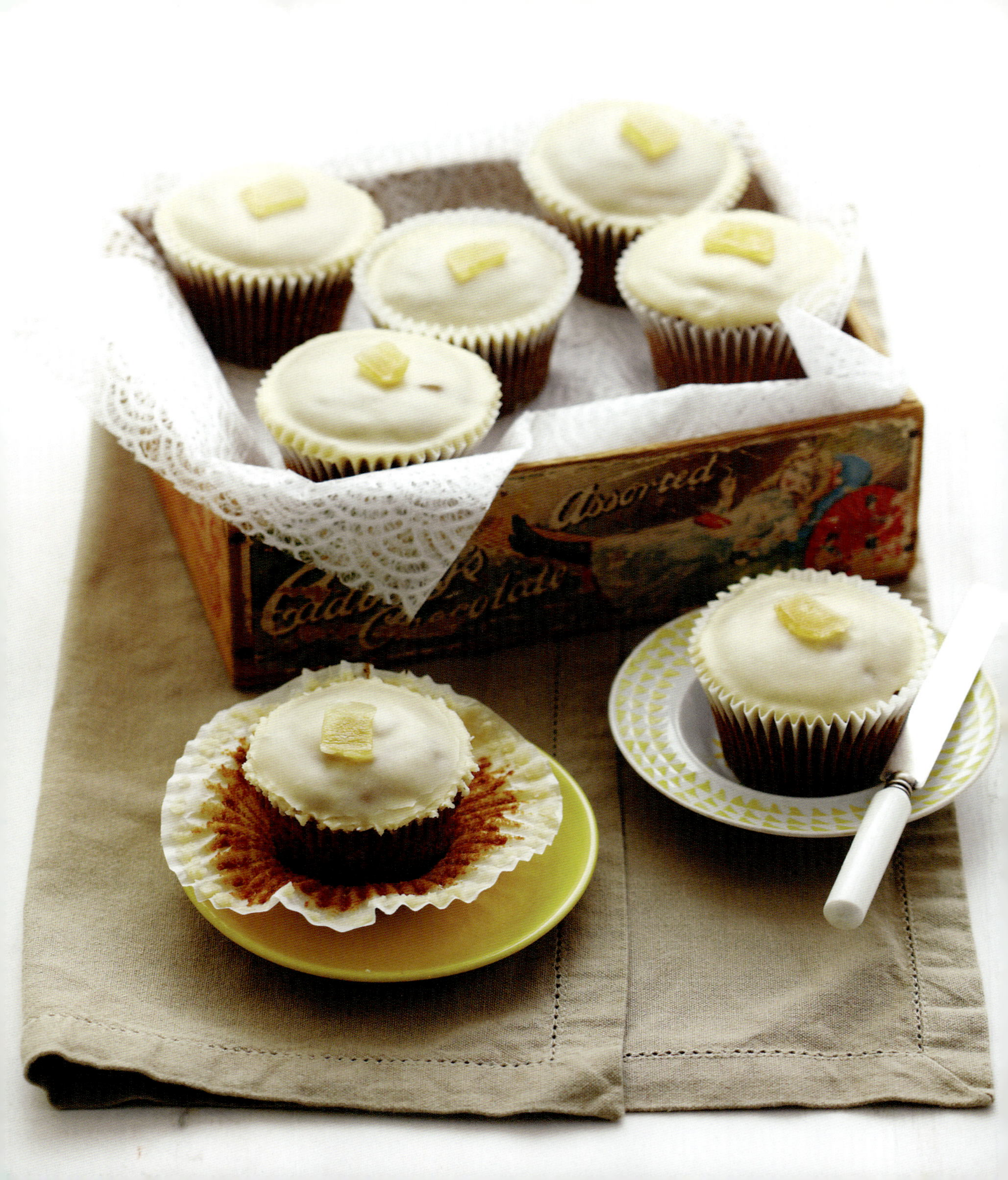
Assorted

Gingerbread cupcakes

Preparation time: 20 minutes
Cooking time: 30 minutes
Decorating time: 10 minutes
Makes: 12 standard cupcakes

235 g (8½ oz/⅔ cup) golden syrup
100 g (3½ oz) unsalted butter, chopped
250 g (9 oz/1⅔ cups) self-raising flour
110 g (3¾ oz/¾ cup) plain flour
½ teaspoon bicarbonate of soda
3 teaspoons ground ginger
1 teaspoon ground cinnamon
1 teaspoon mixed spice
220 g (7¾ oz/1 cup, firmly packed) soft brown sugar
55 g (2 oz/¼ cup) glacé ginger, chopped
250 ml (9 fl oz/1 cup) buttermilk
2 eggs, at room temperature, lightly beaten
sliced glacé ginger, extra, to decorate

Ginger icing
250 g (9 oz/2 cups) pure icing sugar, sifted
1 teaspoon ground ginger
20 g (¾ oz) unsalted butter, softened

TIP: Keep iced and decorated cupcakes in an airtight container in a cool place for up to 2 days.

1 Preheat oven to 190°C (375°F/Gas 5). Line 12 standard (80 ml/2½ fl oz/⅓ cup) muffin holes with paper cases.
2 Put the golden syrup and butter in a small saucepan and stir over medium heat until melted. Remove from the heat and cool. Sift the flours, bicarbonate of soda, ginger, cinnamon and mixed spice into a large bowl. Stir in the brown sugar and chopped glacé ginger. Make a well in the centre.
3 Combine the golden syrup mixture, the buttermilk and egg in a jug and pour into the well in the dry ingredients. Use a large metal spoon to fold in gently until just combined – the mixture should still be lumpy. Divide the mixture evenly among the paper cases.
4 Bake for 20–25 minutes, turning the tin around after 12 minutes, or until a skewer inserted into the centre of a cupcake comes out clean. Allow to cool for 5 minutes in the tin before transferring to a wire rack to cool completely.
5 To make the ginger icing, put the icing sugar, ginger and butter in a small heatproof bowl. Stir in enough warm water to form a smooth paste. Sit the bowl over a saucepan of simmering water, making sure the base of the bowl doesn't touch the water. Stir until smooth and glossy. Remove from the heat.
6 Spread 1½ teaspoons of the icing over each cooled cupcake and top with a glacé ginger slice.

Low-fat berry cupcakes

Preparation time: 20 minutes
Cooking time: 25 minutes
Makes: 12 standard cupcakes

olive or canola oil cooking spray (optional)
185 g (6½ oz/1¼ cups) self-raising flour
1 teaspoon baking powder
1 teaspoon ground cinnamon
35 g (1¼ oz/¼ cup) oat bran
50 g (1¾ oz/½ cup) rolled (porridge) oats
75 g (2¾ oz/⅓ cup) caster sugar
1 egg
425 ml (15 fl oz) buttermilk
60 g (2¼ oz) reduced-fat canola oil margarine, just melted
1 teaspoon vanilla extract
155 g (5½ oz/1 cup) fresh or frozen (unthawed) blueberries
60 g (2¼ oz/½ cup) fresh or frozen (unthawed) raspberries
pure icing sugar, to dust

> **TIPS:** If using frozen berries don't thaw them before adding.
>
> Do not overmix the batter or the cupcakes will be heavy.
>
> Keep cupcakes in an airtight container in the fridge for up to 2 days. Serve at room temperature.

1 Preheat oven to 180°C (350°F/Gas 4). Spray 12 standard (80 ml/2½ fl oz/⅓ cup) muffin holes with oil spray or line with paper cases.
2 Sift the flour, baking powder and cinnamon together into a large bowl. Stir in the oat bran, oats and sugar. Make a well in the centre.
3 Whisk together the egg, buttermilk, melted margarine and vanilla in a medium bowl. Add to the flour mixture with the berries and use a wooden spoon to mix until just combined. Do not overmix – the mixture should still be slightly lumpy. Divide the mixture evenly among the muffin holes or paper cases.
4 Bake for 25 minutes, turning the tin around after 15 minutes, or until firm to the touch and a skewer inserted into the centre of a cupcake comes out clean. Allow to cool for 5 minutes in the tin before transferring to a wire rack.
5 Serve warm or at room temperature dusted with the icing sugar.

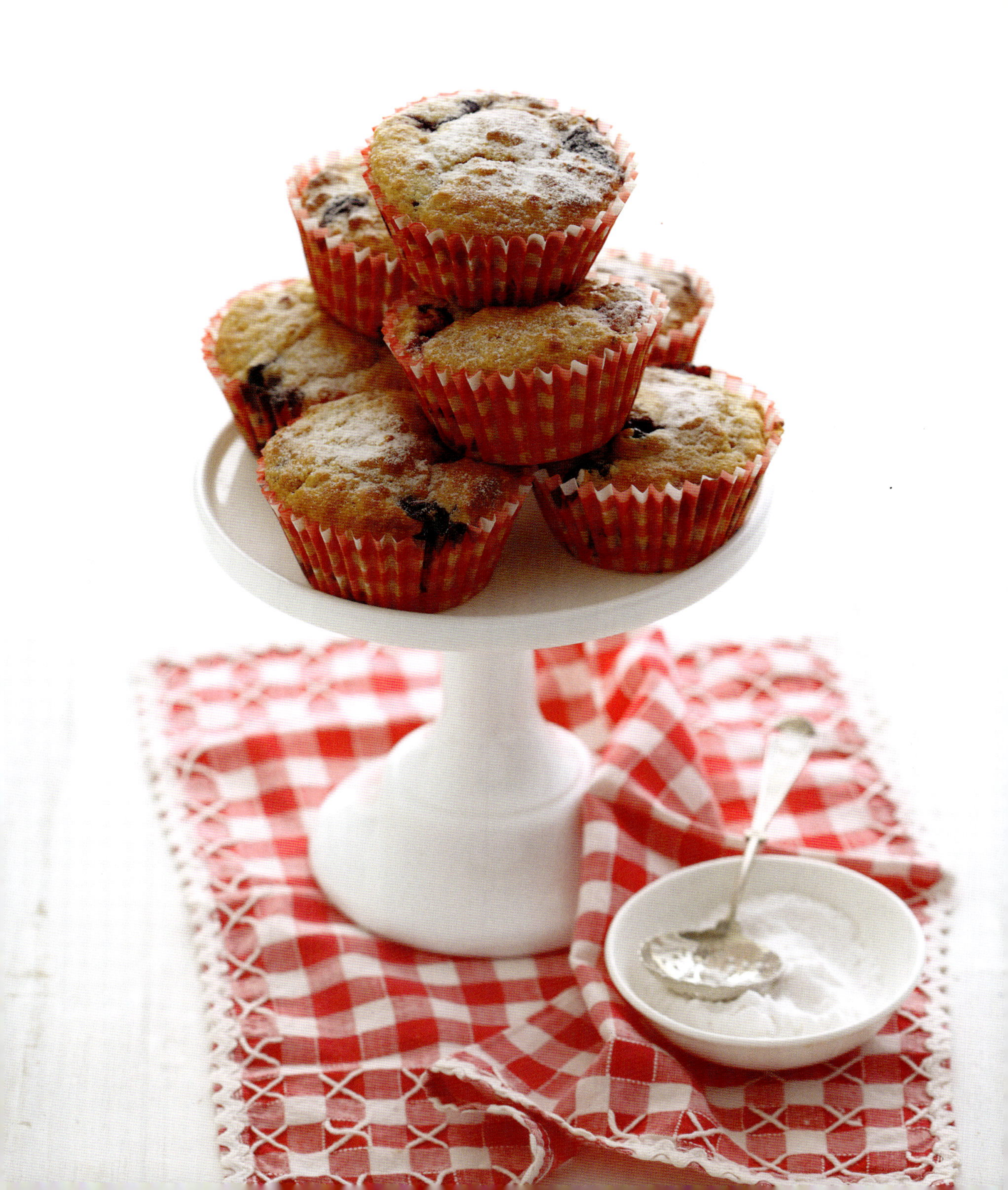

Butterfly cakes

Preparation time: 10 minutes
Cooking time: nil
Decorating time: 25 minutes
Makes: 24 patty pan cupcakes

300 ml (10½ fl oz) thickened (whipping) cream
1 tablespoon pure icing sugar, sifted, plus extra, to dust
¼ teaspoon vanilla extract
24 vanilla patty pan cupcakes (see page 116)
110 g (3¾ oz/⅓ cup) strawberry jam

1 Use electric beaters with a whisk attachment to beat the cream, icing sugar and vanilla in a small bowl until firm peaks form. Use a small, sharp pointed knife to cut a shallow (1 cm/½ in) dome from the top of each cupcake, leaving a small border of cake around the edge. Reserve the cut-out domes.
2 Put ½ teaspoon of jam into the hole in each cupcake and top with a tablespoonful of the cream. Cut the cake domes in half and place on top of the cream to form wings.
3 Dust with the extra icing sugar to serve.

TIPS: Apricot jam or lemon curd can be used in place of the strawberry jam.

Keep undecorated cupcakes in an airtight container in the fridge for up to 2 days.

Variations

Chocolate butterfly cakes: Replace the vanilla patty pan cupcakes with chocolate patty pan cupcakes (see pages 116–117) and use raspberry jam instead of the strawberry jam.

Poppy seed cupcakes with orange syrup

Preparation time: 25 minutes (+ cooling time)
Cooking time: 45 minutes
Makes: 12 standard cupcakes

melted butter, to grease
60 ml (2 fl oz/¼ cup) milk, at room temperature
50 g (1¾ oz/⅓ cup) poppy seeds
185 g (6½ oz/1¼ cups) plain flour
1 teaspoon baking powder
165 g (5¾ oz/¾ cup) caster sugar
185 g (6½ oz) unsalted butter, well softened (see tip)
3 eggs, at room temperature
60 ml (2 fl oz/¼ cup) strained freshly squeezed orange juice
finely grated zest of 1 orange

Orange syrup
2 oranges, lemons and limes
220 g (7¾ oz/1 cup) caster sugar
125 ml (4 fl oz/½ cup) strained freshly squeezed orange juice
125 ml (4 fl oz/½ cup) water

> **TIPS:** Beat soft butter for 1 minute with electric beaters until well softened.
>
> Serve cupcakes warm with thick (double/heavy) cream or vanilla ice cream. Drizzle with a little of the reserved syrup.
>
> Keep cupcakes (topped with the syrup and zest) in an airtight container in the fridge for up to 2 days. Serve at room temperature.

1 Preheat oven to 160°C (315°F/Gas 2–3). Grease 12 standard (80 ml/2½ fl oz/⅓ cup) muffin holes.
2 Combine the milk and poppy seeds in a small bowl. Sift the flour and baking powder into a large bowl. Add the sugar, butter and eggs. Use electric beaters to mix on low speed for 30 seconds or until combined. Add the orange juice and beat until just combined and smooth. Use a large metal spoon to stir through the orange zest, and milk and poppy seed mixture.
3 Divide the mixture evenly among the muffin holes then tap on the bench to smooth.
4 Bake for 35 minutes on the lowest shelf in the oven, turning the tin around after 20 minutes, or until golden and a skewer inserted into the centre of a cupcake comes out clean. Allow to cool for 10 minutes in the tin.
5 Meanwhile, to make the syrup, remove the zest from the fruit using a zester. Put the sugar, orange juice and water in a small saucepan over high heat, and stir until the sugar dissolves. Add the zest, increase the heat to high and boil for 10 minutes or until the syrup is slightly reduced.
6 Transfer the cupcakes to a baking tray. Use a thin skewer to prick eight small holes around the centre of each cupcake. Spoon the syrup, without the zest, over the cakes, reserving about 2 tablespoons with the zest. Place a small pile of the zest mixture on top of each cupcake. Serve warm or at room temperature.

Passionfruit cupcakes

Preparation time: 20 minutes
Cooking time: 20 minutes
Decorating time: 15 minutes
Makes: 14 standard cupcakes

185 g (6½ oz) unsalted butter, softened
165 g (5¾ oz/¾ cup) caster sugar
1 teaspoon vanilla extract
3 eggs, at room temperature
125 g (4½ oz) cream cheese, softened
1 tablespoon fresh passionfruit pulp (see tip)
150 g (5½ oz/1 cup) self-raising flour
35 g (1¼ oz/¼ cup) plain flour
60 ml (2 fl oz/¼ cup) milk

Topping
300 ml (10½ fl oz) thickened (whipping) cream
1½ tablespoons pure icing sugar, sifted
4 passionfruit, pulp only

TIPS: You will need about 1 passionfruit to give 1 tablespoon of pulp.

Keep undecorated cupcakes in an airtight container in a cool place for up to 2 days. Decorate just before serving.

1 Preheat oven to 180°C (350°F/Gas 4). Line 14 standard (80 ml/2½ fl oz/⅓ cup) muffin holes with paper cases.

2 Use an electric mixer to beat the butter, sugar and vanilla together in a medium bowl until pale and creamy. Add the eggs, one at a time, beating well after each addition. Add the cream cheese and passionfruit pulp and beat until smooth. Sift the flours together. Use a large metal spoon or spatula to fold in the flours and milk alternately in two separate batches each. Beat on low speed until just combined. Divide the mixture evenly among the paper cases.

3 Bake for 20 minutes or until a skewer inserted into the centre of a cupcake comes out clean. Allow to cool for 5 minutes in the tins before transferring to a wire rack to cool completely.

4 To make the topping, use electric beaters with a whisk attachment, or a balloon whisk, to whisk the cream and icing sugar together in a medium bowl until firm peaks form.

5 Use a small, sharp pointed knife to cut a round out of each cupcake, leaving a 1 cm (½ in) border. Discard the cut-out pieces. Spoon the cream into a piping bag fitted with a 1 cm (½ in) star nozzle. To decorate, pipe a rosette of cream into the hole in each cupcake and then spoon over a little of the passionfruit pulp.

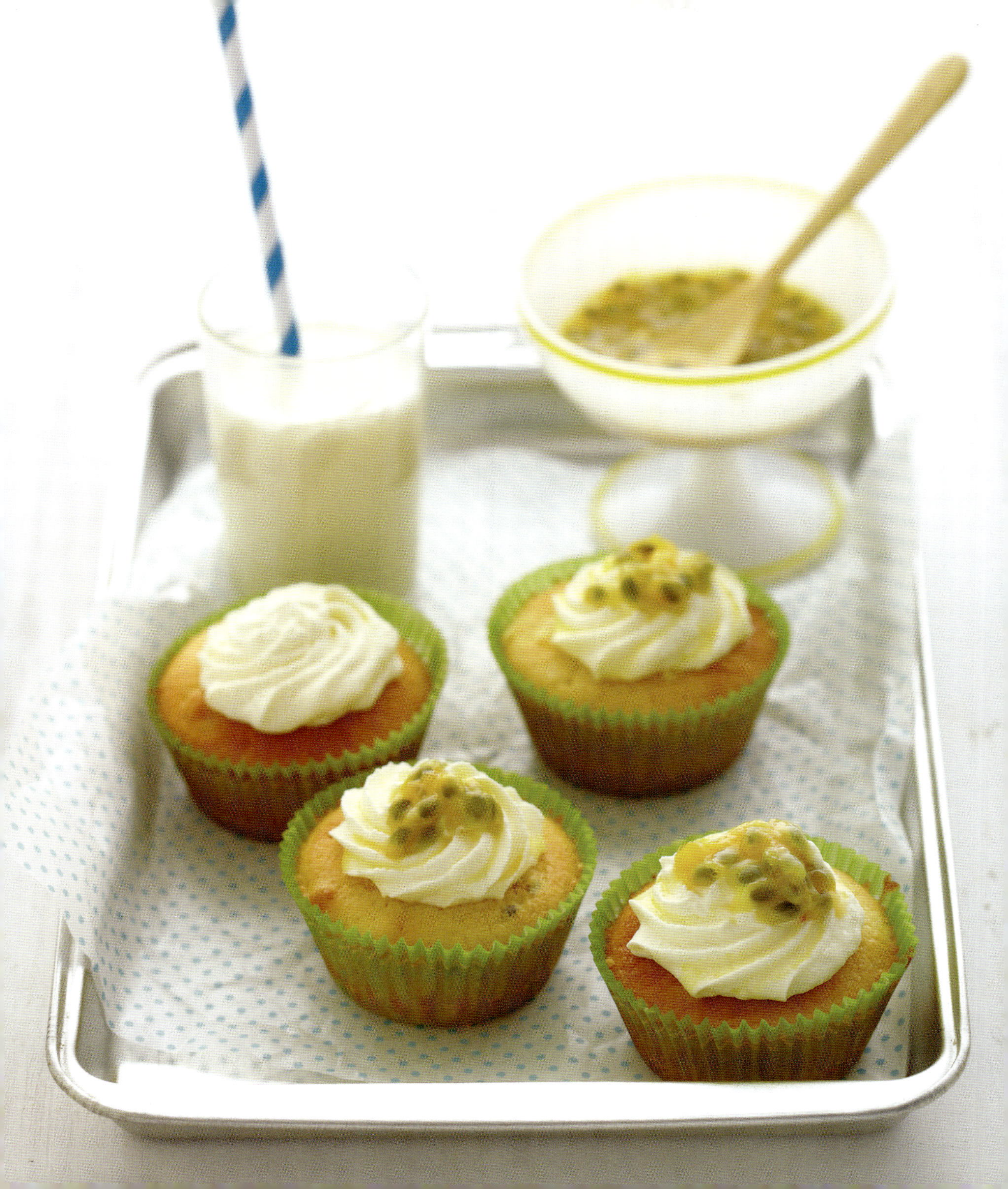

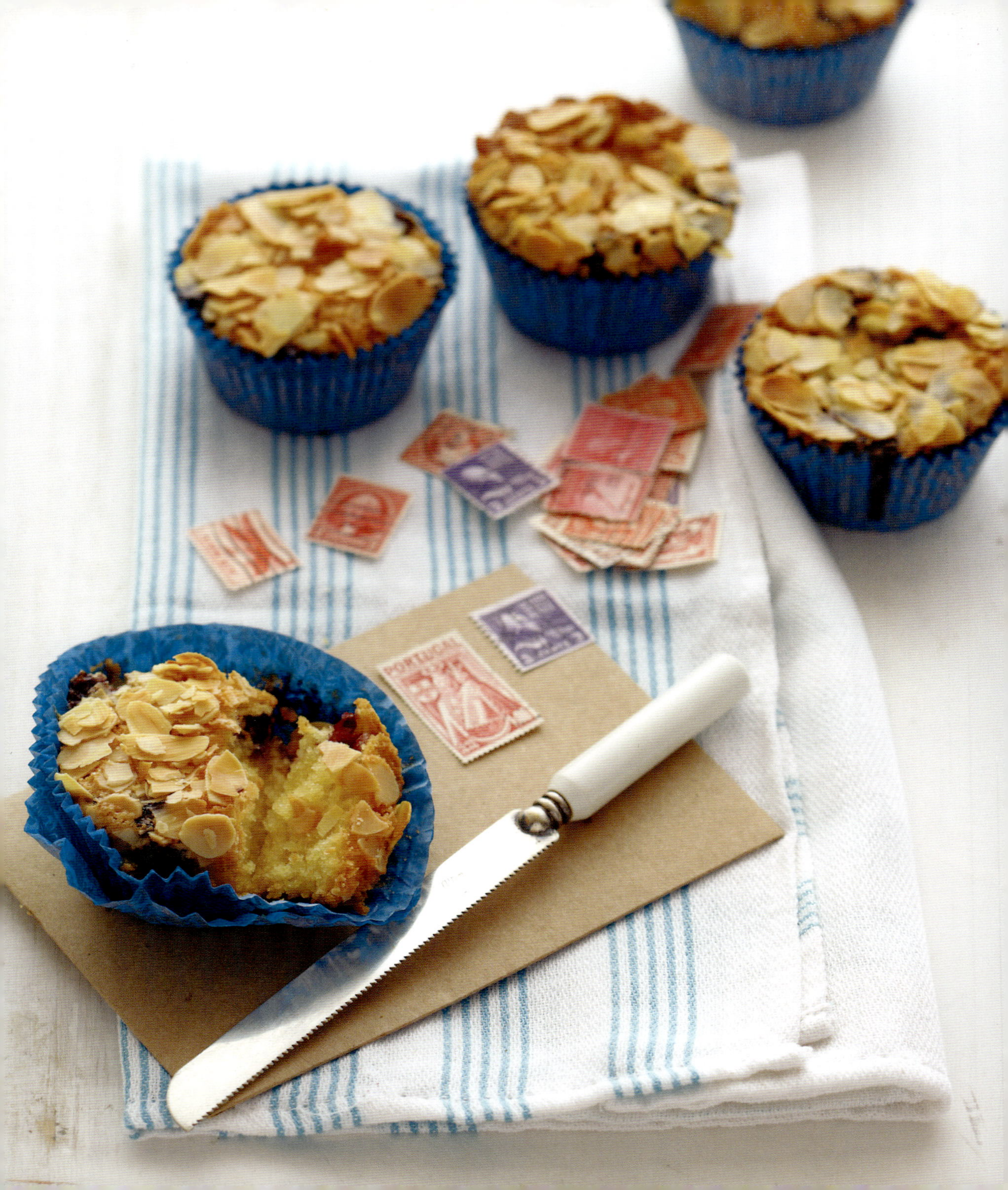
PORTUGAL

Blueberry semolina cakes

Preparation time: 15 minutes
Cooking time: 30 minutes
Makes: 7 standard cupcakes

> 35 g (1¼ oz/¼ cup) self-raising flour
> 65 g (2½ oz/⅓ cup) fine semolina
> 220 g (7¾ oz/1 cup) caster sugar
> 25 g (1 oz/¼ cup) almond meal
> ½ teaspoon finely grated lemon zest
> 4 egg whites, at room temperature, lightly beaten
> 125 g (4½ oz) unsalted butter, melted, cooled
> 80 g (2¾ oz/½ cup) fresh or frozen (unthawed) blueberries (see tip)
> 35 g (1¼ oz/⅓ cup) flaked almonds
> pure icing sugar, to dust (optional)

1 Preheat oven to 170°C (325°F/Gas 3). Line 7 standard (80 ml/2½ fl oz/⅓ cup) muffin holes with paper cases.
2 Sift the flour and semolina into a large bowl and add the sugar, almond meal and lemon zest. Stir to combine. Add the egg white and use electric beaters to mix until combined. Pour in the melted butter and continue to beat until smooth and well combined. Add the blueberries and fold through with a wooden spoon to just combine.
3 Divide the mixture evenly among the paper cases and sprinkle with the flaked almonds.
4 Bake for 30 minutes or until a skewer inserted into the centre of a cupcake comes out clean. Allow to cool for 5 minutes in the tin before transferring to a wire rack to cool completely.
5 Dust with the icing sugar, if using, to serve.

> **TIPS:** You can use mixed berries or raspberries in place of the blueberries. If using frozen berries don't thaw them before adding.
>
> These cupcakes are best served on the day of making.

Just for kids

Ice cream sundae cupcakes

Preparation time: 15 minutes (+ 1 hour cooling time)
Cooking time: nil
Decorating time: 5 minutes
Makes: 6 large cupcakes

>6 large vanilla cupcakes (see page 116)
>500 ml (17 fl oz/2 cups) strawberry ice cream
>2 tablespoons roasted unsalted peanuts, chopped
>
>**Chocolate sauce**
>40 g (1½ oz/⅓ cup) unsweetened cocoa powder, sifted
>100 ml (3½ fl oz) water
>75 g (2¾ oz/⅓ cup) caster sugar
>20 g (¾ oz) dark chocolate, chopped

1 To make the chocolate sauce, put all the ingredients in a small saucepan and stir over low heat until the sugar dissolves, the chocolate melts and the sauce is smooth. Transfer to a bowl and set aside for 1 hour to cool to room temperature.
2 Use a small, sharp pointed knife to cut a cone shape about 4.5 cm (1¾ in) in diameter out of the top of each cupcake (this will hold the ice cream in place). Discard the cut-out pieces.
3 To decorate, put a scoop of the ice cream on top of each cake. Drizzle with a little of the cooled chocolate sauce and sprinkle with the peanuts. Serve immediately with the remaining sauce passed separately.

> **TIP:** Keep any leftover chocolate sauce in an airtight container in the fridge for up to 2 weeks. Serve with ice cream or add 60 ml (2 fl oz/¼ cup) sauce to 250 ml (9 fl oz/ 1 cup) milk then shake or blend for a rich milkshake.

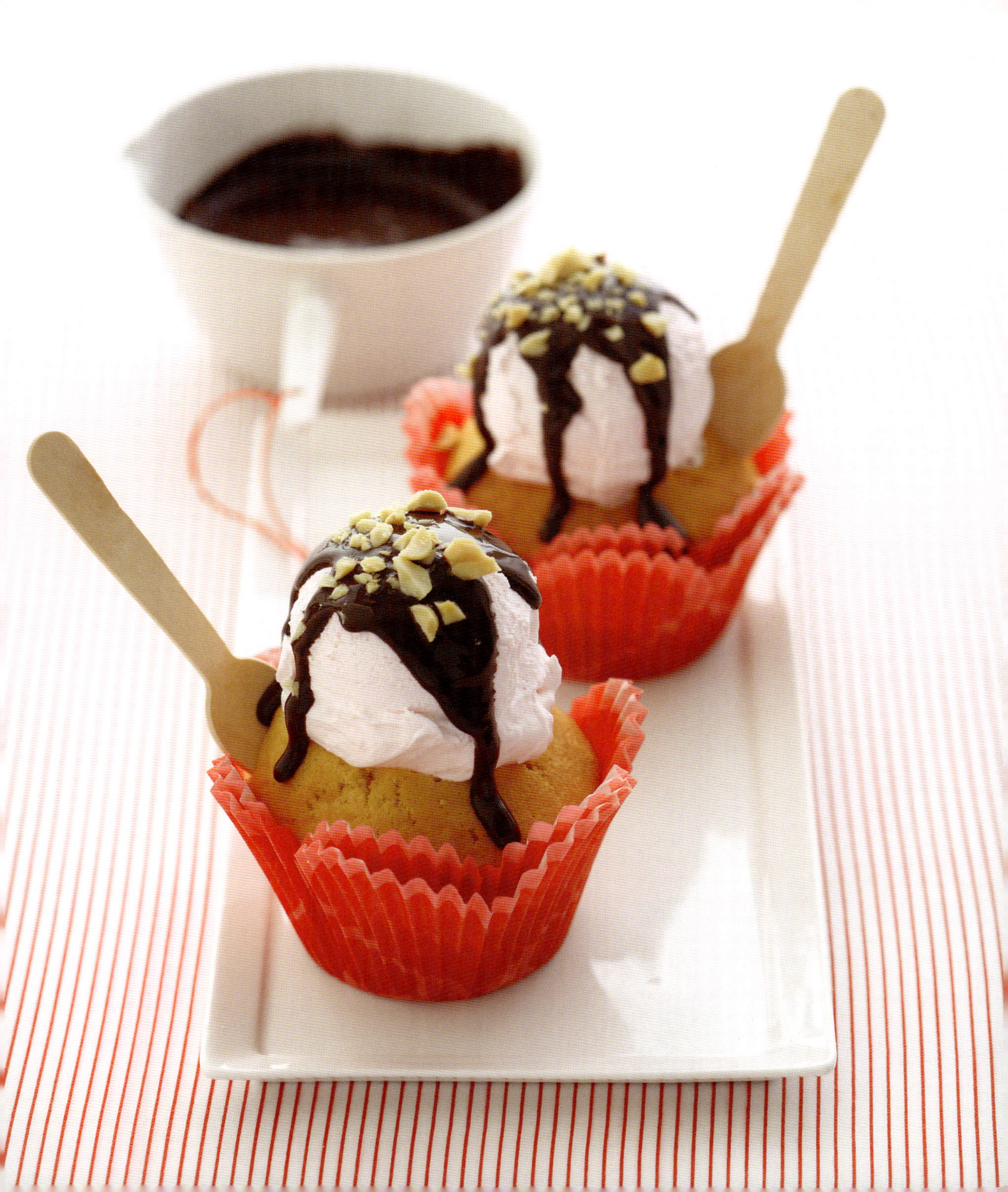

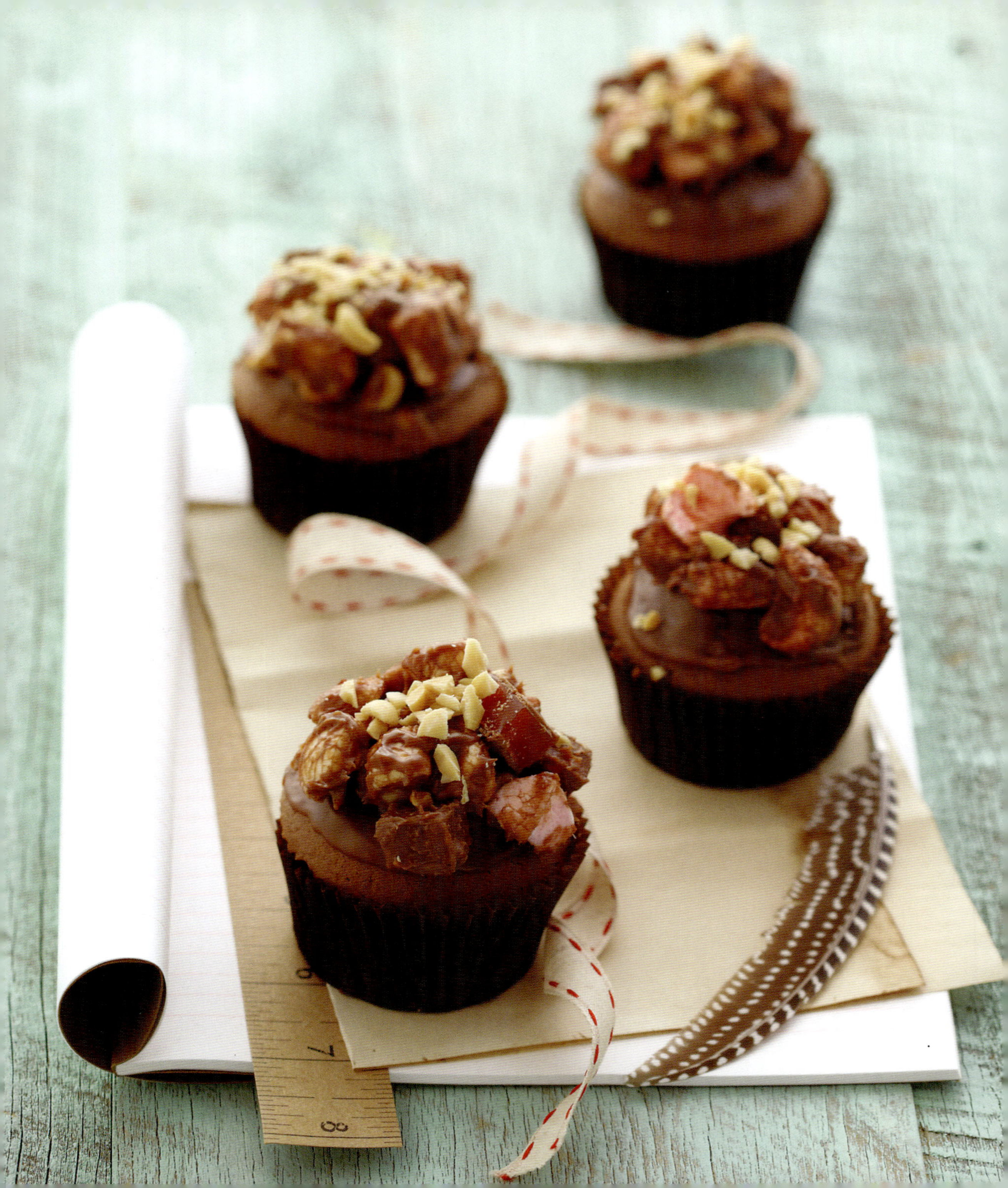

Rocky road cupcakes

Preparation time: 15 minutes (+ cooling time + 30 minutes chilling time)
Cooking time: nil
Decorating time: 10 minutes
Makes: 12 standard cupcakes

200 g (7 oz) milk chocolate, chopped
100 ml (3½ fl oz) thickened (whipping) cream
2 x 65 g (2½ oz) chocolate-coated Turkish delight bars, cut into 1 cm (½ in) cubes
100 g (3½ oz) marshmallows, chopped
40 g (1½ oz/¼ cup) coarsely chopped peanuts
12 standard chocolate cupcakes (see pages 116–117)

TIP: Keep decorated cupcakes in an airtight container in the fridge for up to 2 days. Serve at room temperature.

1 Put the chocolate in a large heatproof bowl. Put the cream in a small saucepan, bring to the boil, remove from the heat and pour over the chocolate. Allow to stand for 30 seconds, then stir gently until the chocolate melts. Set aside until cooled to room temperature then remove 125 ml (4 fl oz/½ cup) of the chocolate mixture and set aside.
2 Add the Turkish delight, marshmallows and 2 tablespoons of the peanuts to the remaining chocolate mixture and stir to lightly coat.
3 To decorate, spread the reserved chocolate mixture over the tops of the cupcakes, top with the Turkish delight mixture and sprinkle with the remaining peanuts. Refrigerate for 30 minutes or until the topping is set.

This little piggy

Preparation time: 20 minutes
Cooking time: 20 minutes
Decorating time: 40 minutes
Makes: 24 patty pan cupcakes

- 125 g (4½ oz) unsalted butter, softened
- 150 g (5½ oz/⅔ cup) caster sugar
- 85 g (3 oz/⅔ cup) packet strawberry jelly crystals
- 3 eggs, at room temperature
- 225 g (8 oz/1½ cups) plain flour
- 1½ teaspoons baking powder
- 60 ml (2 fl oz/¼ cup) milk
- ½ quantity vanilla buttercream (see page 123)
- pink food colouring
- 500 g (1 lb 2 oz) packet large marshmallows (pink ones only) (see tip)
- 100 g (3½ oz) packet mini candy-coated chocolate buttons (brown and pink ones only) (see tip)

TIPS: You will need to buy this quantity of marshmallows and candy-coated chocolate buttons but use only the colours specified.

Keep iced and decorated cupcakes in an airtight container in the fridge for up to 2 days. Serve at room temperature.

1 Preheat oven to 170°C (325°F/Gas 3). Line 24 flat-based (40 ml/1¼ fl oz) patty pan holes with paper cases.

2 Use an electric mixer to beat the butter, sugar and jelly crystals together in a medium bowl until paler and creamy. Add the eggs, one at a time, beating well after each addition. Sift the flour and baking powder into a bowl. With the mixer on low speed, add the flour and milk alternately in two separate batches each. Beat on low speed until just combined. Divide the mixture evenly among the paper cases.

3 Bake for 20 minutes, turning the tins around after 10 minutes, or until golden and a skewer inserted into the centre of a cupcake comes out clean. Allow to cool for 5 minutes in the tins before transferring to a wire rack to cool completely.

4 To decorate, tint the buttercream with the pink food colouring to desired colour and spread over the tops of the cooled cupcakes. Cut a pink marshmallow in half, pinch each half to form ears and place at the top of a cake. Cut another pink marshmallow in half and use half for the nose. Decorate with the brown candy-coated chocolate buttons for the eyes and the pink candy-coated chocolate buttons for the nose. Repeat with the remaining cupcakes, marshmallows and candy-coated chocolate buttons.

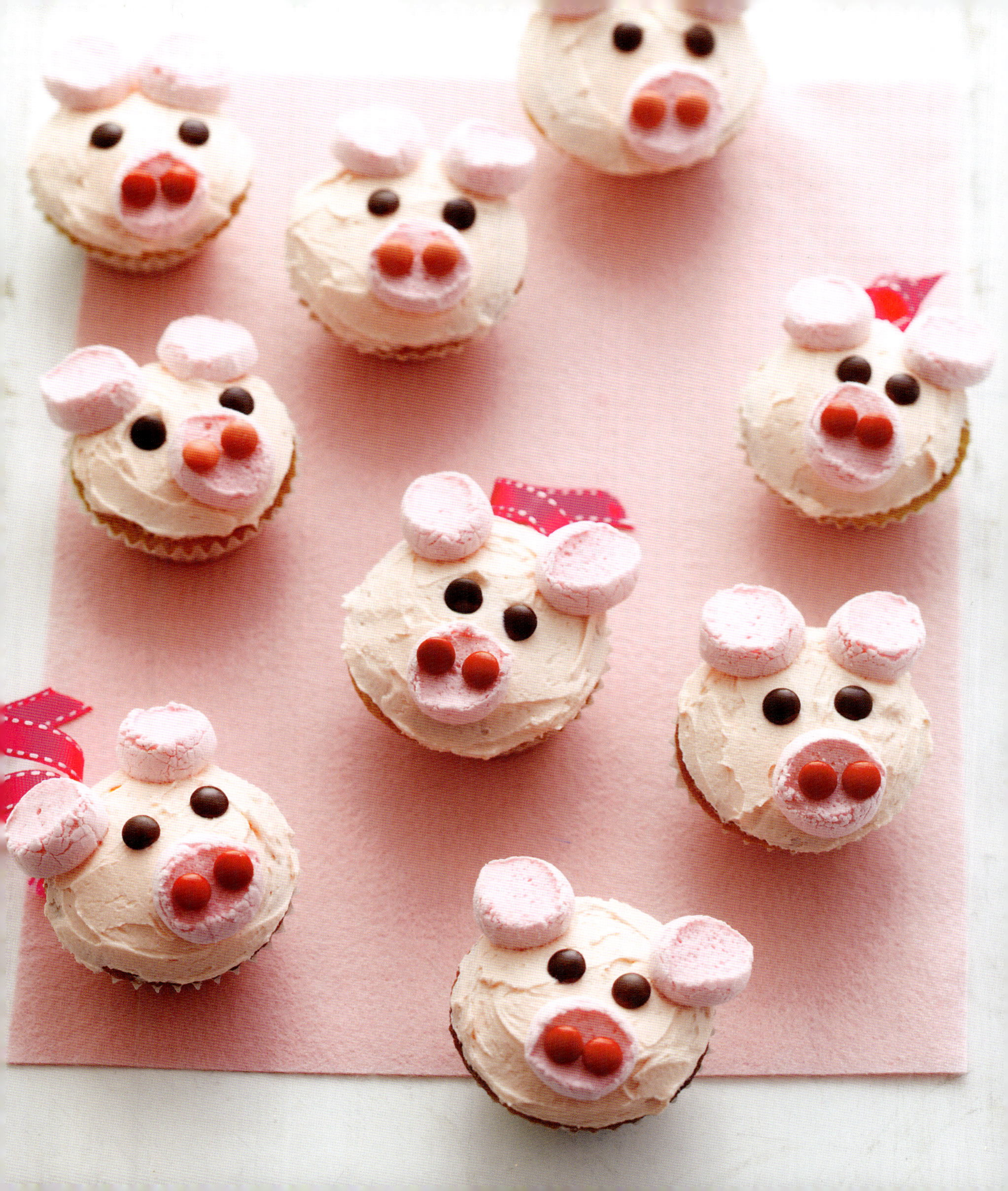

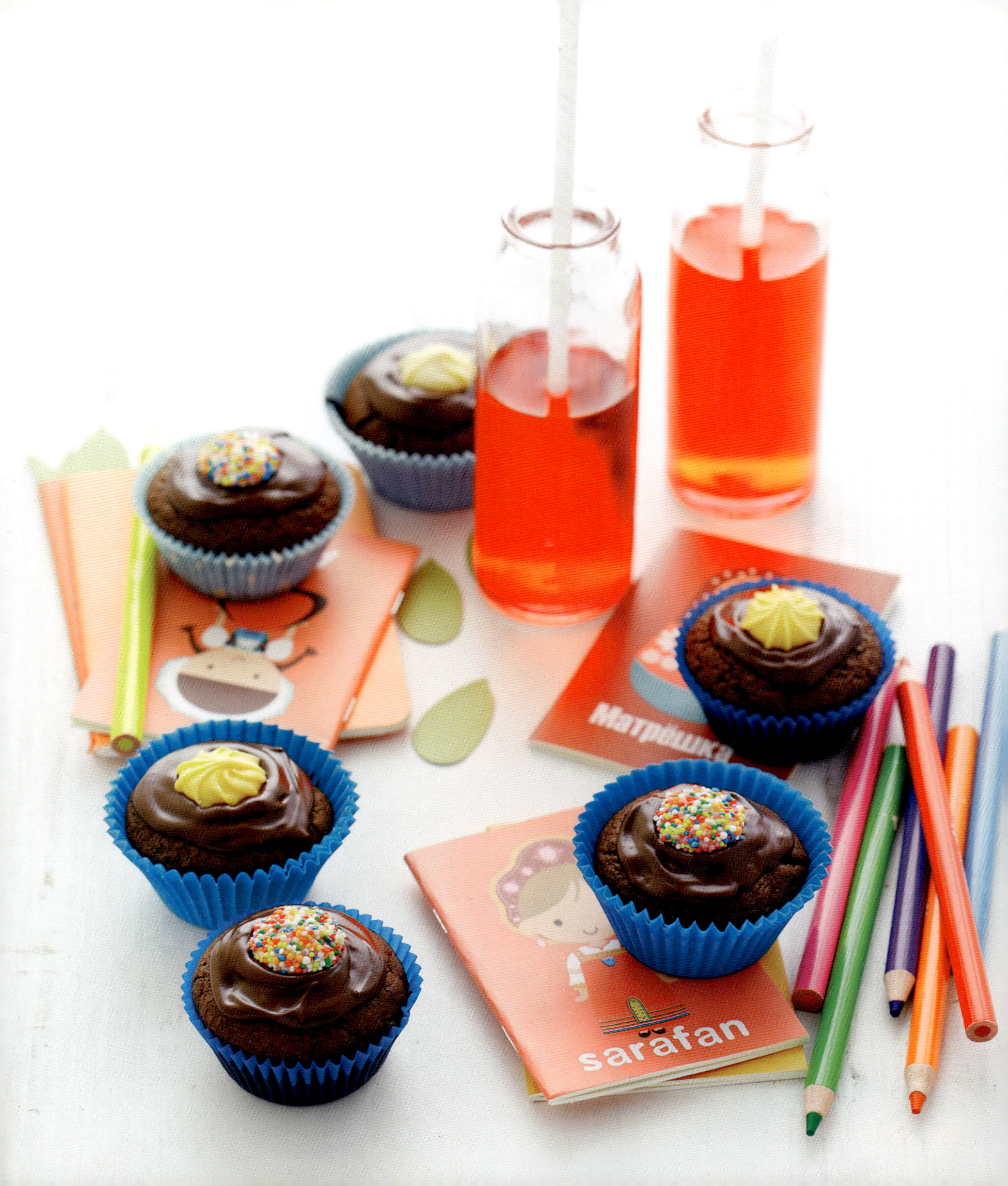
sarafan

Triple chocolate brownie cupcakes

Preparation time: 30 minutes (+ 30 minutes cooling time + 1½ hours standing time)
Cooking time: 25 minutes
Decorating time: 15 minutes
Makes: 12 standard cupcakes

225 g (8 oz) dark chocolate, chopped
110 g (3¾ oz) unsalted butter, chopped
220 g (7¾ oz/1 cup, firmly packed) soft brown sugar
3 eggs, at room temperature, lightly beaten
1 teaspoon vanilla extract
75 g (2¾ oz/½ cup) plain flour
¼ teaspoon baking powder
30 g (1 oz/¼ cup) unsweetened cocoa powder
12 mixed chocolate buttons

Chocolate fudge icing
200 g (7 oz) dark chocolate, chopped
25 g (1 oz) unsalted butter, well softened
2 tablespoons golden syrup

TIP: Keep iced and decorated cupcakes in an airtight container in the fridge for up to 2 days. Serve at room temperature.

1 Preheat oven to 180°C (350°F/Gas 4). Line 12 standard (80 ml/2½ fl oz/⅓ cup) muffin holes with paper cases.
2 Put the chocolate and butter in a medium heatproof bowl over a saucepan of simmering water, making sure the base of the bowl doesn't touch the water. Stir frequently until melted and smooth. Remove from the heat. Transfer the chocolate mixture to a large bowl, taking care not to let any condensation from the bowl drip into the mixture.
3 Add the sugar, egg and vanilla to the chocolate mixture and use a balloon whisk to whisk until combined. Sift the flour, baking powder and cocoa powder over the top and whisk until combined. Divide the mixture evenly among the paper cases.
4 Bake for 20–25 minutes, turning the tin around after 15 minutes. (The cupcakes are ready when the mixture sticking to a skewer forms a soft ball when rolled between your thumb and forefinger.) Allow to cool for 30 minutes in the tin before transferring to a wire rack to cool completely.
5 To make the chocolate fudge icing, put the dark chocolate in a small heatproof bowl over a saucepan of simmering water, making sure the base of the bowl doesn't touch the water. Stir frequently until melted and smooth. Remove the pan from the heat (leaving the bowl over the water) add the butter and golden syrup and stir until combined.
6 To decorate, spoon a tablespoon of fudge icing onto the centre of each cupcake and use a teaspoon to spread it into a neat circle on top of the cupcake. Top each cupcake with a chocolate button.
7 Serve immediately or set aside at room temperature for 1½ hours until the icing is set.

Peanut butter cupcakes

Preparation time: 20 minutes
Cooking time: 25 minutes
Decorating time: 15 minutes
Makes: 12 friand-shaped or standard cupcakes

225 g (8 oz/1½ cups) plain flour
1½ teaspoons baking powder
220 g (7¾ oz/1 cup) caster sugar
125 g (4½ oz) unsalted butter, softened
60 g (2¼ oz/¼ cup) smooth peanut butter
60 ml (2 fl oz/¼ cup) milk
3 eggs, at room temperature
1 teaspoon vanilla extract
40 g (1½ oz) dark chocolate, shaved with a sharp knife

Peanut butter cream
60 g (2¼ oz/¼ cup) smooth peanut butter
60 g (2¼ oz) unsalted butter, just softened
1 tablespoon milk
1½ teaspoons vanilla extract
125 g (4½ oz/1 cup) pure icing sugar, sifted

TIP: Keep iced and decorated cupcakes in an airtight container in the fridge for up to 2 days. Serve at room temperature.

1 Preheat oven to 170°C (325°F/Gas 3). Line 12 friand (125 ml/4 fl oz/½ cup) holes with friand paper cases or 12 standard (80 ml/2½ fl oz/⅓ cup) muffin holes with paper cases.
2 Sift the flour and baking powder into a large bowl. Add the sugar, butter, peanut butter, milk, eggs and vanilla. Use electric beaters to beat on low speed until combined. Increase speed to medium and beat for 2–3 minutes until well combined, very smooth and paler in colour. Divide the mixture evenly among the paper cases then smooth the tops with the back of a teaspoon.
3 Bake for 20–25 minutes, turning the tin around after 15 minutes, or until golden and a skewer inserted into the centre of a cupcake comes out clean. Allow to cool for 5 minutes in the tin before transferring to a wire rack to cool completely.
4 To make the peanut butter cream, use electric beaters to beat the peanut butter and butter in a small bowl for 1 minute or until pale and creamy. Add the milk, vanilla and half the icing sugar and beat until well combined. Add the remaining icing sugar and beat for 1–2 minutes or until smooth and creamy.
5 To decorate, spread the peanut butter cream onto the cooled cupcakes. Sprinkle with the shaved chocolate.

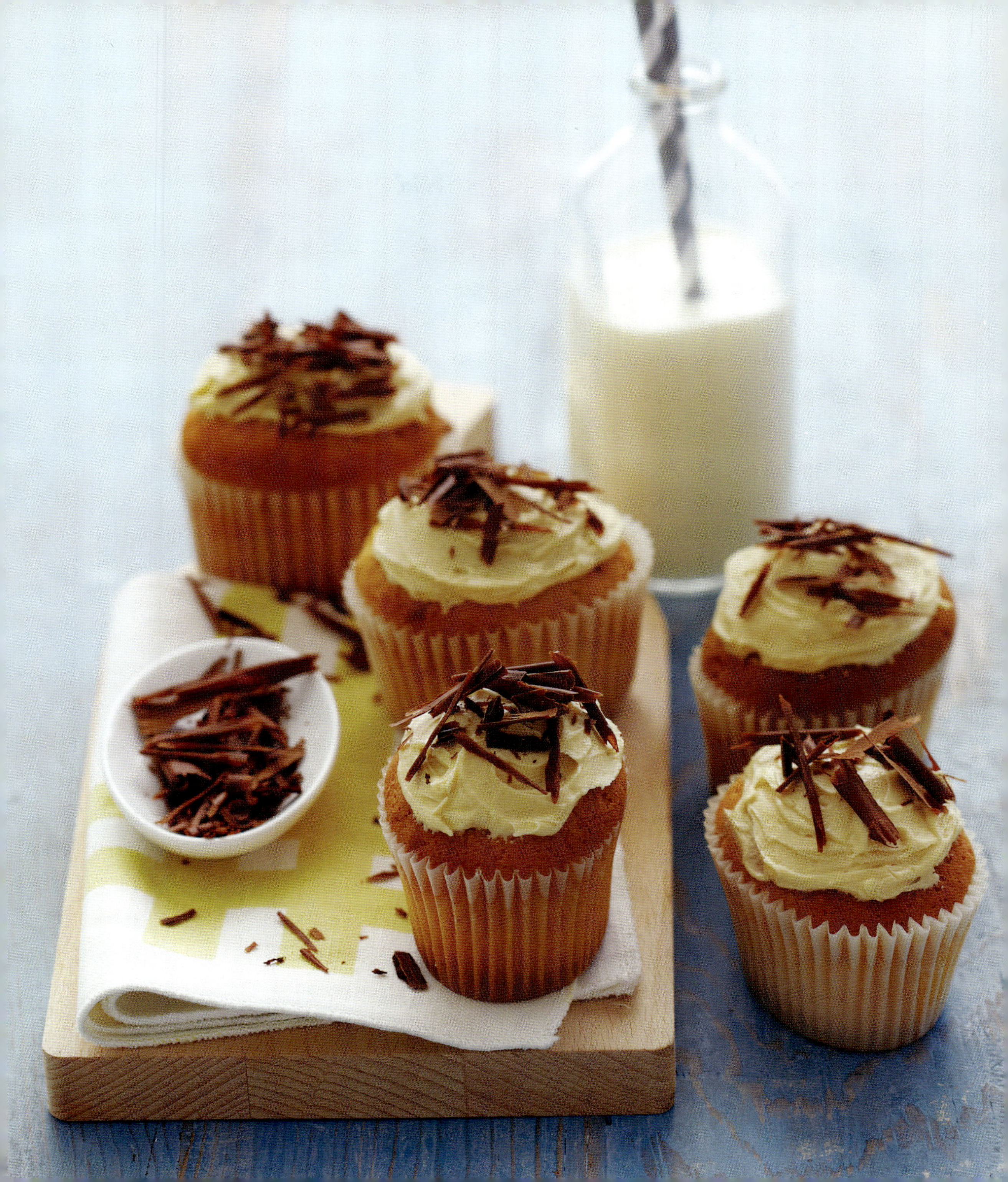

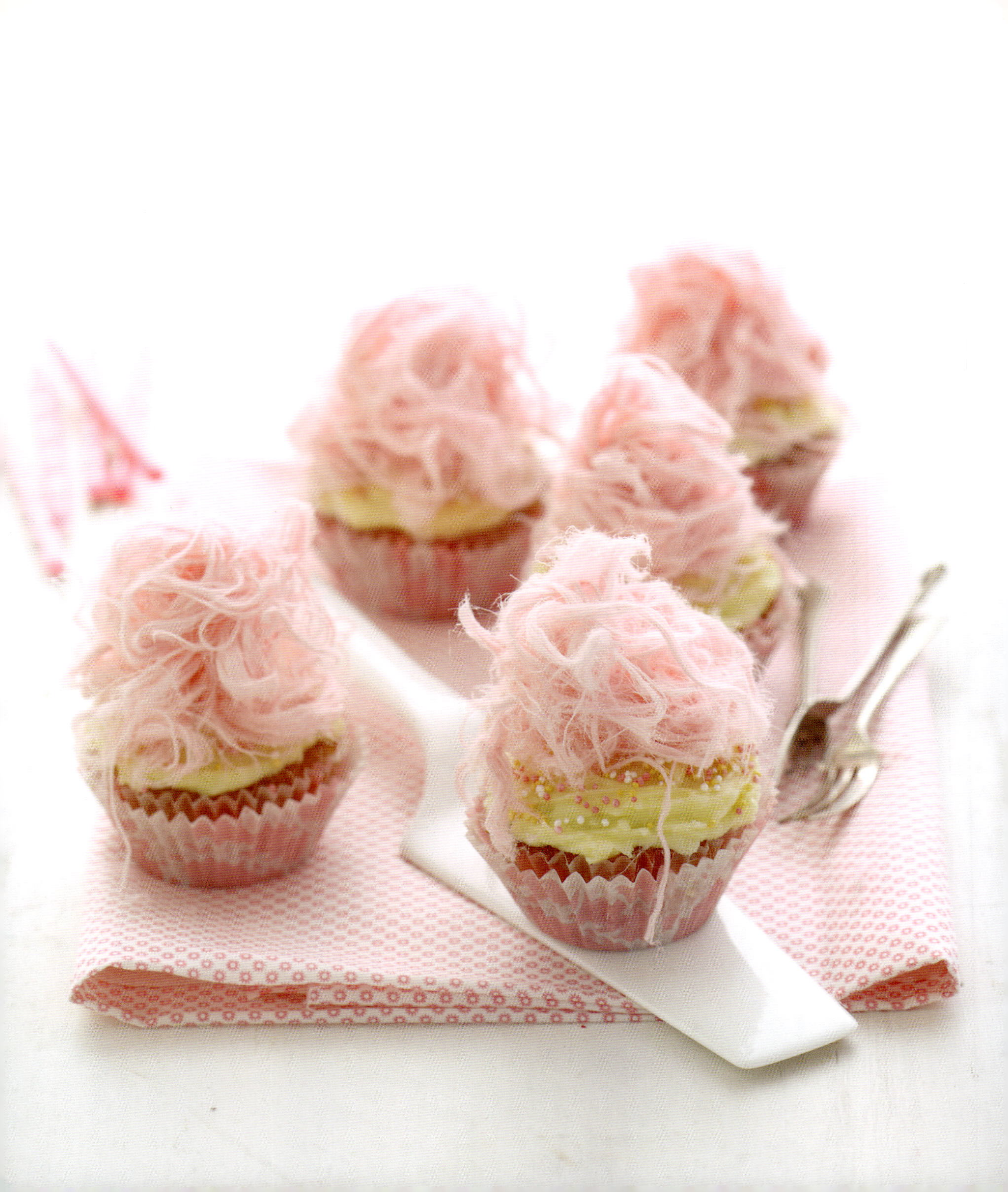

Pretty in pink

Preparation time: 25 minutes (+ 2–3 hours standing time)
Cooking time: 40 minutes
Decorating time: 15 minutes
Makes: 12 standard cupcakes

- 150 g (5½ oz) unsalted butter, softened
- 165 g (5¾ oz/¾ cup) caster sugar
- 2 eggs, at room temperature
- 185 g (6½ oz/1¼ cups) self-raising flour, sifted
- 80 ml (2½ fl oz/⅓ cup) buttermilk
- 40 g (1½ oz/⅓ cup) fresh or frozen raspberries, partially thawed if frozen, lightly crushed
- 400 g (14 oz) white chocolate, chopped
- 160 ml (5¼ fl oz) thickened (whipping) cream
- 2 tablespoons coloured sprinkles
- 100 g (3½ oz) pink fairy floss

TIPS: Decorate the cupcakes with the fairy floss just before serving. Store any leftover floss in an airtight container.

The white chocolate topping can be made up to 1 day ahead and kept covered in the fridge. Just before using, microwave for a few seconds to soften slightly.

Keep iced and decorated cupcakes (without the fairy floss) in an airtight container in the fridge for up to 2 days. Serve at room temperature.

1 Preheat oven to 180°C (350°F/Gas 4). Line 12 standard (80 ml/2½ fl oz/⅓ cup) muffin holes with paper cases.

2 Use an electric mixer to beat the butter and sugar together in a medium bowl until pale and creamy. Add the eggs, one at a time, beating well after each addition. Use a large metal spoon or spatula to fold in the flour and buttermilk alternately in two separate batches each. Add the raspberries and gently swirl through the mixture. Divide the mixture evenly among the paper cases then smooth the tops with the back of a teaspoon.

3 Bake for 35 minutes, turning the tin around after 20 minutes, or until golden and a skewer inserted into the centre of a cupcake comes out clean. Allow to cool for 5 minutes in the tin before transferring to a wire rack to cool completely.

4 Meanwhile, put the chocolate in a medium heatproof bowl. Put the cream in a small saucepan, bring to the boil, remove from the heat and pour over the chocolate. Stand for 30 seconds, then stir gently until the chocolate melts. Cover and set aside for 2–3 hours or until set.

5 To decorate, spread the white chocolate mixture over the tops of the cooled cupcakes. Sprinkle with coloured sprinkles and top with the fairy floss.

Choc-hazelnut cupcakes

Preparation time: 35 minutes
Cooking time: 25 minutes
Decorating time: 15 minutes
Makes: 12 standard cupcakes

225 g (8 oz/1½ cups) plain flour
1½ teaspoons baking powder
165 g (5¾ oz/¾ cup) caster sugar
125 g (4½ oz) unsalted butter, softened
60 ml (2 fl oz/¼ cup) milk
3 eggs, at room temperature
1 teaspoon vanilla extract
80 g (2¾ oz/¼ cup) chocolate-hazelnut spread

Choc-hazelnut icing
125 g (4½ oz) unsalted butter, just softened
105 g (3½ oz/⅓ cup) chocolate-hazelnut spread
2 tablespoons milk
3 teaspoons vanilla extract
250 g (9 oz/2 cups) pure icing sugar, sifted
2 tablespoons unsweetened cocoa powder, sifted

1 Preheat oven to 160°C (315°F/Gas 2–3). Line 12 standard (80 ml/2½ fl oz/⅓ cup) muffin holes with paper cases
2 Sift the flour and baking powder into a large bowl. Add the sugar, butter, milk, eggs and vanilla. Use electric beaters to beat on low speed until combined. Increase speed to medium–high and beat for 2–3 minutes until well combined, very smooth and paler in colour.
3 Divide the mixture evenly among the paper cases until halfway full. Top each with 1 teaspoon of the chocolate-hazelnut spread. Top with the remaining cupcake mixture then smooth the tops with the back of a teaspoon.
4 Bake for 20–25 minutes, turning the tin around after 15 minutes, or until golden and the top of a cupcake springs back when gently pressed. Allow to cool for 5 minutes in the tin before transferring to a wire rack to cool completely.
5 To make the choc-hazelnut icing, use electric beaters to beat the butter and chocolate-hazelnut spread in a medium bowl for 1 minute or until pale and creamy. Add the milk, vanilla and half the icing sugar and beat until well combined. Add the remaining icing sugar and the cocoa powder. Beat for 1–2 minutes or until smooth and creamy.
6 To decorate, use a piping bag fitted with a 1 cm (½ in) fluted nozzle to pipe the frosting into joined-together dots on the tops of the cooled cupcakes.

TIP: Keep iced cupcakes in an airtight container in the fridge for up to 2 days. Serve at room temperature.

Chocolate chip cupcakes

Preparation time: 20 minutes
Cooking time: 25 minutes
Decorating time: 15 minutes
Makes: 12 standard cupcakes

>melted butter, to grease (optional)
>225 g (8 oz/1½ cups) plain flour
>1½ teaspoons baking powder
>165 g (5¾ oz/¾ cup) caster sugar
>125 g (4½ oz) unsalted butter, softened
>60 ml (2 fl oz/¼ cup) milk
>3 eggs, at room temperature
>1 teaspoon vanilla extract
>200 g (7 oz/1¼ cups) milk chocolate chips
>½ quantity chocolate buttercream (see page 123)
>50 g (1¾ oz/¼ cup) candy stars or candy-coated chocolate buttons

TIP: Keep iced and decorated cupcakes in an airtight container in the fridge for up to 2 days. Serve at room temperature.

1 Preheat oven to 160°C (315°F/Gas 2–3). Grease or line 12 standard (80 ml/2½ fl oz/⅓ cup) muffin holes with paper cases.
2 Sift the flour and baking powder into a large bowl. Add the sugar, butter, milk, eggs and vanilla. Use electric beaters to beat on low speed until combined. Increase speed to medium–high and beat for 2–3 minutes or until well combined, very smooth and paler in colour. Add the chocolate chips and use a large metal spoon to stir until evenly distributed. Divide the mixture evenly among the muffin holes or paper cases then smooth the tops with the back of a teaspoon.
3 Bake for 20–25 minutes, turning the tin around after 15 minutes, or until golden and a skewer inserted into the centre of a cupcake comes out clean. Allow to cool for 5 minutes in the tin before transferring to a wire rack to cool completely.
4 To decorate, use a spatula to spread the buttercream over the cooled cupcakes. Top with the candy stars or candy-coated chocolate buttons.

Lickable cone cakes

Preparation time: 25 minutes (+ 20 minutes standing time)
Cooking time: 20 minutes
Decorating time: 30 minutes
Makes: 18 ice cream cone cupcakes

18 flat-based ice cream cones
125 g (4½ oz) unsalted butter, softened
165 g (5¾ oz/¾ cup) caster sugar
3 eggs, at room temperature
225 g (8 oz/1½ cups) plain flour
1½ teaspoons baking powder
60 ml (2 fl oz/¼ cup) milk
125 g (4½ oz) milk chocolate, melted, plus
    125 g (4½ oz) milk chocolate, melted, extra
½ quantity vanilla buttercream (see page 123)
coloured sprinkles, to decorate

TIP: These cupcakes are best served on the day of making.

1 Preheat oven to 180°C (350°F/Gas 4). Put the ice cream cones in 18 flat-based (40 ml/1¼ fl oz) patty pan holes.
2 Use an electric mixer to beat the butter and sugar in a medium bowl until pale and creamy. Add the eggs, one at a time, beating well after each addition. Sift the flour and baking powder into a large bowl. With the mixer on low speed, add the flour and milk alternately in two separate batches each. Beat on low speed until just combined. Use a large metal spoon to gently fold the melted chocolate through the mixture to create a rippled effect.
3 Use a large piping bag without a tube, with the end snipped off to make a 1 cm (½ in) hole, to pipe the mixture into the cones until three-quarters full.
4 Bake for 18–20 minutes or until golden and a skewer inserted into the centre of a cupcake comes out clean. Allow to cool for 5 minutes in the tins before transferring to a wire rack to cool completely.
5 To decorate, trim the edges of the cupcakes to neaten if necessary. Spread the buttercream on top of the cooled cupcakes to cover. Drizzle with the extra melted chocolate and sprinkle with coloured sprinkles. Set aside for 20 minutes or until the chocolate is set.

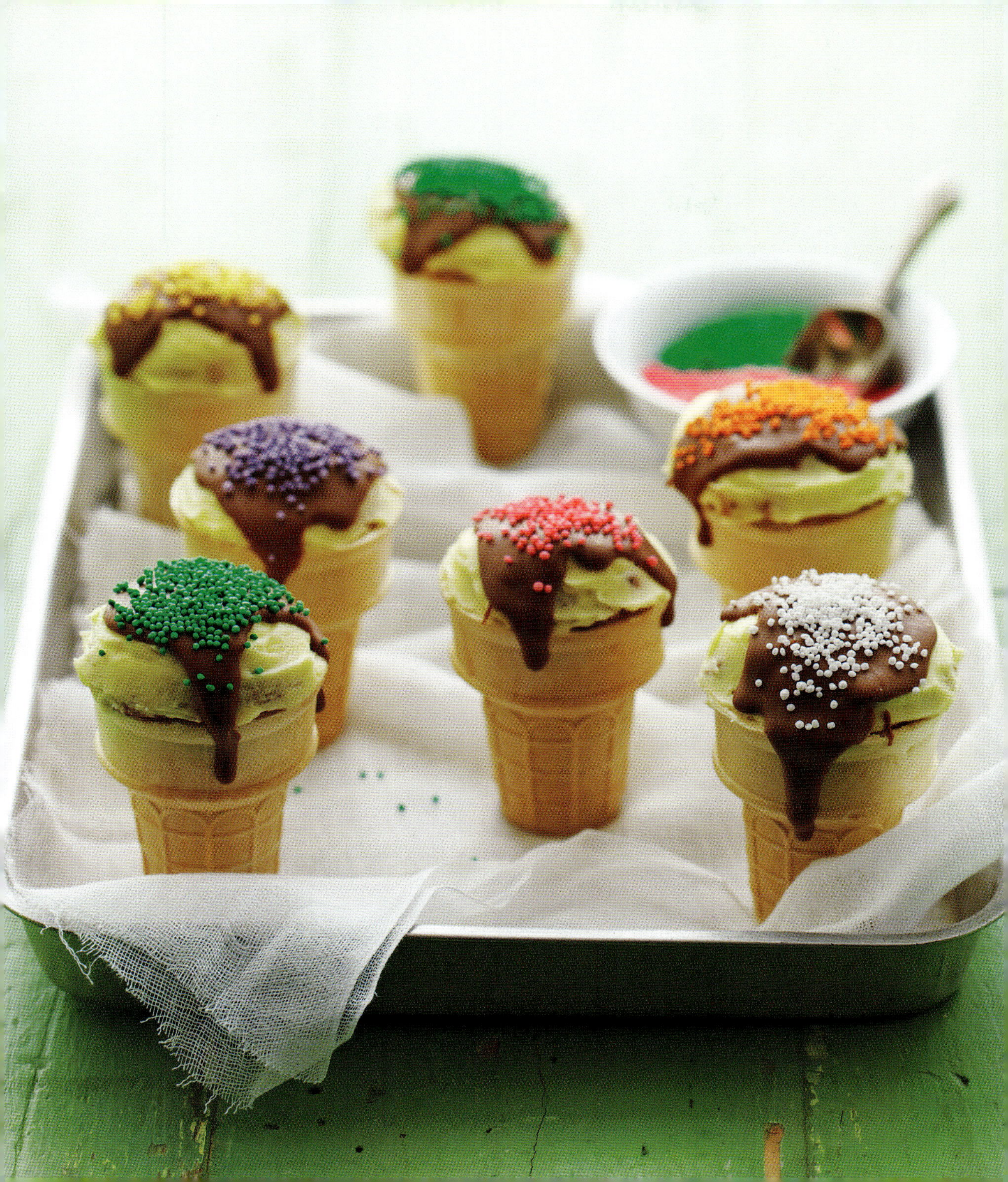

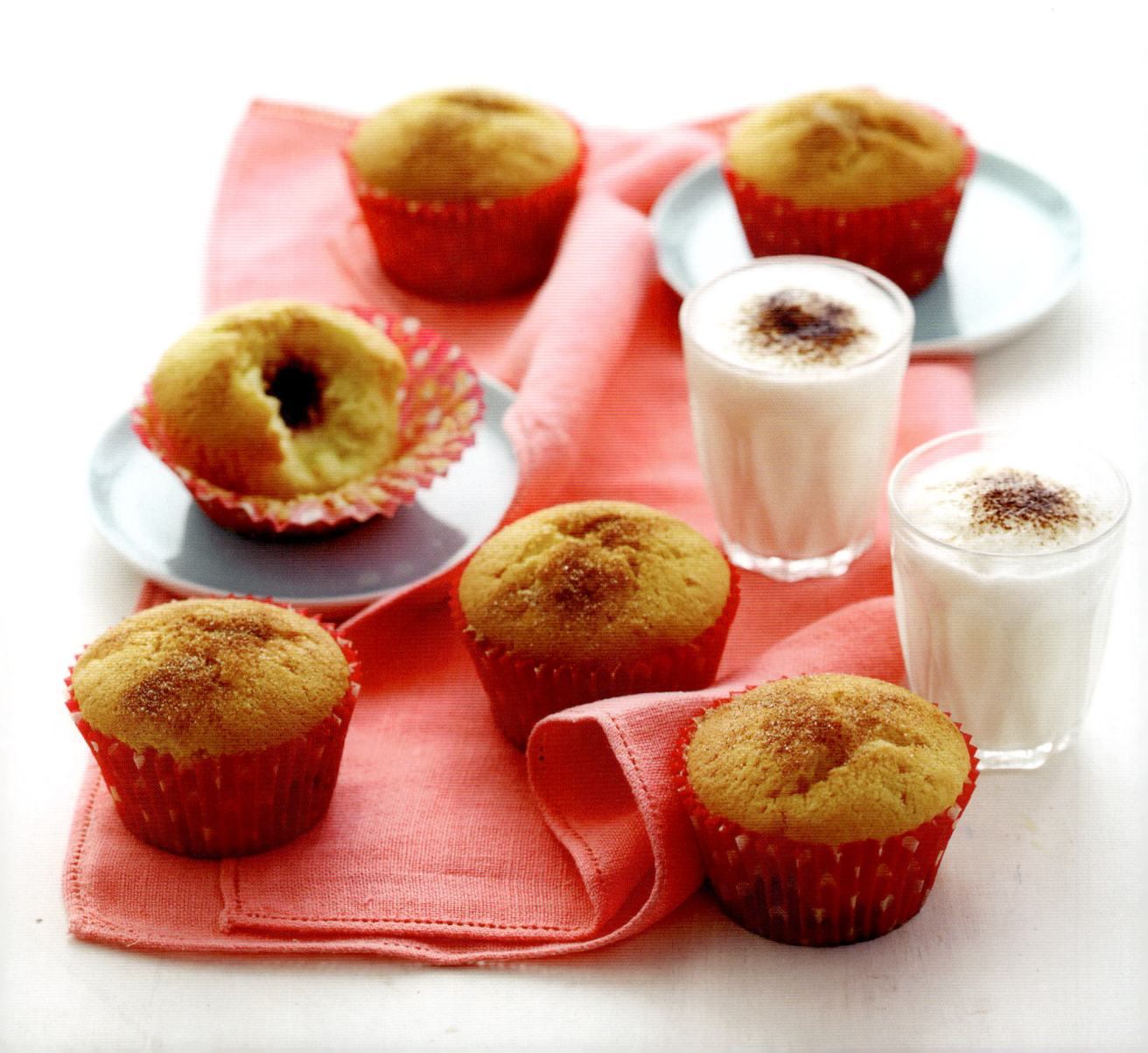

Jam doughnut cupcakes

Preparation time: 25 minutes
Cooking time: 20 minutes
Decorating time: 5 minutes
Makes: 12 standard cupcakes

> 225 g (8 oz/1½ cups) plain flour
> 1½ teaspoons baking powder
> 165 g (5¾ oz/¾ cup) caster sugar
> 125 g (4½ oz) unsalted butter, chopped, softened
> 60 ml (2 fl oz/¼ cup) milk
> 3 eggs, at room temperature
> 1 teaspoon vanilla extract
> 165 g (5¾ oz/½ cup) strawberry jam
> 2 tablespoons cinnamon sugar (see tip)
> 20 g (¾ oz/1 tablespoon) unsalted butter, melted

TIPS: You can make your own cinnamon sugar by mixing 1 tablespoon caster sugar with 1 teaspoon ground cinnamon.

These cupcakes are best served on the day of making.

1 Preheat oven to 160°C (315°F/Gas 2–3). Line 12 standard (80 ml/2½ fl oz/⅓ cup) muffin holes with paper cases.
2 Sift the flour and baking powder into a large bowl. Add the sugar, butter, milk, eggs and vanilla. Use electric beaters to beat on low speed until combined. Increase speed to medium–high and beat for 2–3 minutes or until well combined, very smooth and paler in colour.
3 Divide half the mixture evenly among the paper cases (it will be just enough to cover the bases). Top each with a teaspoon of jam, then cover with the remaining mixture. Tap the tin on the bench to level the mixture.
4 Bake for 20 minutes, turning the tin around after 10 minutes, or until the top of a cupcake springs back when gently pressed.
5 To decorate, brush a little of the melted butter over each hot cupcake, then sprinkle with the cinnamon sugar. Allow to cool for 5 minutes in the tin before transferring to a wire rack. Serve warm.

Baby bears

Preparation time: 20 minutes
Cooking time: 20 minutes
Decorating time: 50 minutes
Makes: 24 patty pan cupcakes

- 125 g (4½ oz) unsalted butter, softened
- 75 g (2¾ oz/⅓ cup) caster sugar
- 175 g (6 oz/½ cup) honey
- 3 eggs, at room temperature
- 225 g (8 oz/1½ cups) plain flour
- 1½ teaspoons baking powder
- 60 ml (2 fl oz/¼ cup) milk, plus extra
- 160 g (5¾ oz) milk chocolate melts (you will need 48)
- ½ quantity vanilla buttercream (see page 123)
- 30 g (1 oz/¼ cup) unsweetened cocoa powder, sifted
- 100 g (3½ oz/2 cups) chocolate puffed rice cereal
- 24 red or brown candy-coated chocolate buttons
- 70 g (2½ oz) yellow mini candy-coated chocolate buttons

TIP: Keep iced and decorated cupcakes in an airtight container in the fridge for up to 1 day. Serve at room temperature.

1 Preheat oven to 170°C (350°F/Gas 4). Line 24 flat-based (40 ml/1¼ fl oz) patty pan holes with paper cases.

2 Use an electric mixer to beat the butter, sugar and honey together in a medium bowl until pale and creamy. Add the eggs, one at a time, beating well after each addition. Sift the flour and baking powder into a medium bowl. With the mixer on low speed, add the flour and milk alternately in two separate batches each. Beat on low speed until just combined. Divide the mixture evenly among the paper cases then smooth the tops with the back of a teaspoon.

3 Bake for 15–20 minutes, turning the tins around after 10 minutes, or until golden and a skewer inserted into the centre of a cupcake comes out clean. Allow to cool for 5 minutes in the tins before transferring to a wire rack to cool completely.

4 To decorate, carefully cut 24 of the chocolate melts in half for the ears. Reserve 2 tablespoons of the buttercream. Beat the cocoa powder into the remaining buttercream, adding a little extra milk if needed. Reserve 3 tablespoons of the chocolate buttercream, put in a piping bag and snip off the end. Put the chocolate puffed rice cereal in a bowl. Spread the cooled cupcakes with the remaining chocolate buttercream, add 2 chocolate melt halves for ears then gently press the cupcakes into the chocolate puffed rice cereal to cover. Use a little of the reserved chocolate buttercream to attach the remaining chocolate melts for the nose, then to attach the candy-coated chocolate buttons to the nose and the mini buttons for the eyes. Put the reserved vanilla buttercream in a piping bag, snip a little off the end and pipe the mouths. Pipe the centres of the eyes with the chocolate buttercream.

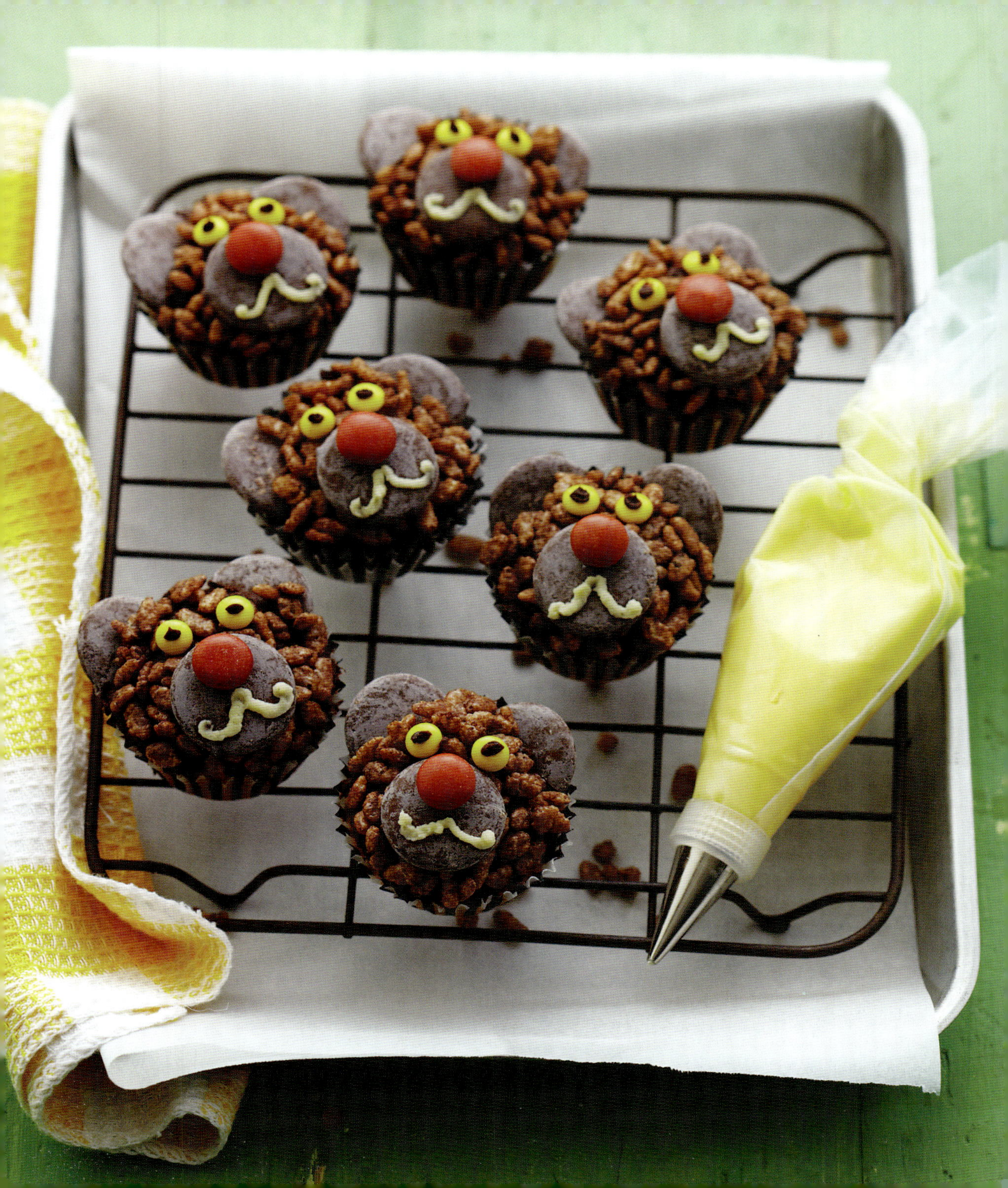

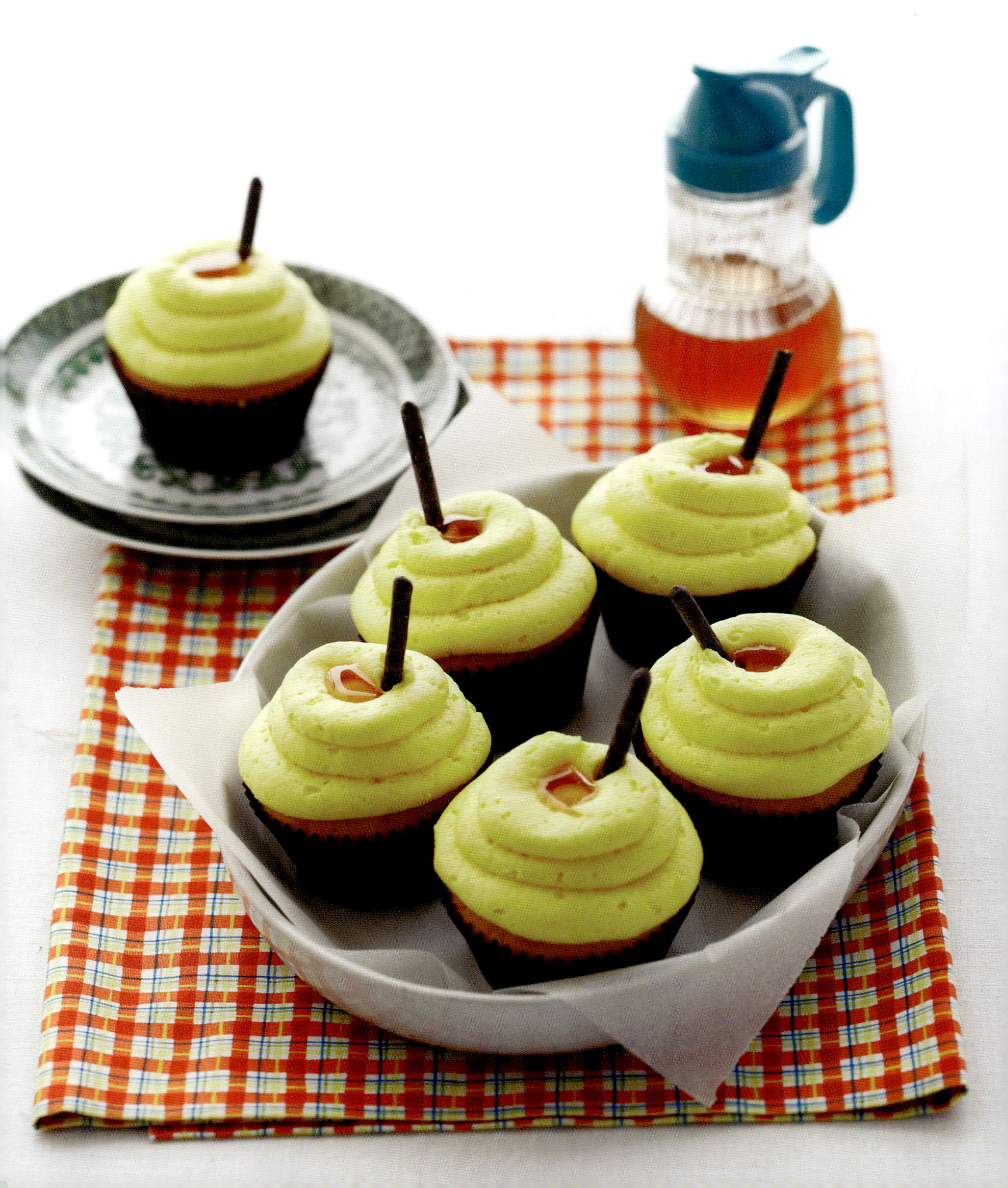

Honey pot cupcakes

Preparation time: 10 minutes
Cooking time: nil
Decorating time: 25 minutes
Makes: 12 standard cupcakes

12 standard vanilla cupcakes (see page 116), baked in brown paper cases
125 ml (4 fl oz/½ cup) thick (double/heavy) cream
2½ tablespoons creamed honey
1 quantity vanilla buttercream (see page 123), tinted with yellow food colouring to desired colour
2 tablespoons honey, to decorate
6 chocolate sticks, halved

1 Use a small, sharp pointed knife to cut a 3 cm (1¼ in) diameter hole in the top of each cake. Discard the cut-out tops.
2 Put the cream and creamed honey in a medium bowl and gently and slowly whisk to combine until the honey is dissolved, then whisk to soft peaks. Use a piping bag fitted with an 11 mm (½ in) plain nozzle to pipe the honey cream into the cupcake holes.
3 Use a piping bag fitted with a 11 mm (½ in) plain nozzle to pipe the buttercream on top of the cupcakes in a beehive-shaped swirl, leaving a hole in the centre.
4 Use a small teaspoon to drizzle a little of the honey into the hole in the buttercream. Add a chocolate stick to each honey pot.

TIP: Keep iced and decorated cupcakes in an airtight container in the fridge for up to 2 days. Serve at room temperature.

Funny faces

Preparation time: 10 minutes
Cooking time: nil
Decorating time: 30 minutes
Makes: 12 standard cupcakes

> 12 standard vanilla cupcakes (see page 116)
> 1 quantity cream cheese frosting (see page 120)
> selection of assorted lollies (such as raspberry-flavoured frogs, musk lollies, ring-shaped hard candies, candy-coated chocolate buttons, jelly beans, fruit-flavoured soft candies, jelly babies, licorice allsorts, mini boiled lollies and fairy floss), to decorate

1 Level the tops of the cupcakes if necessary. Spread with the frosting.
2 Decorate with the lollies to make faces as shown or as desired.

TIPS: Decorate these cupcakes just before serving.

These cupcakes are perfect ones for kids to decorate at a child's party. Have the cupcakes already iced and let the kids create their own funny faces.

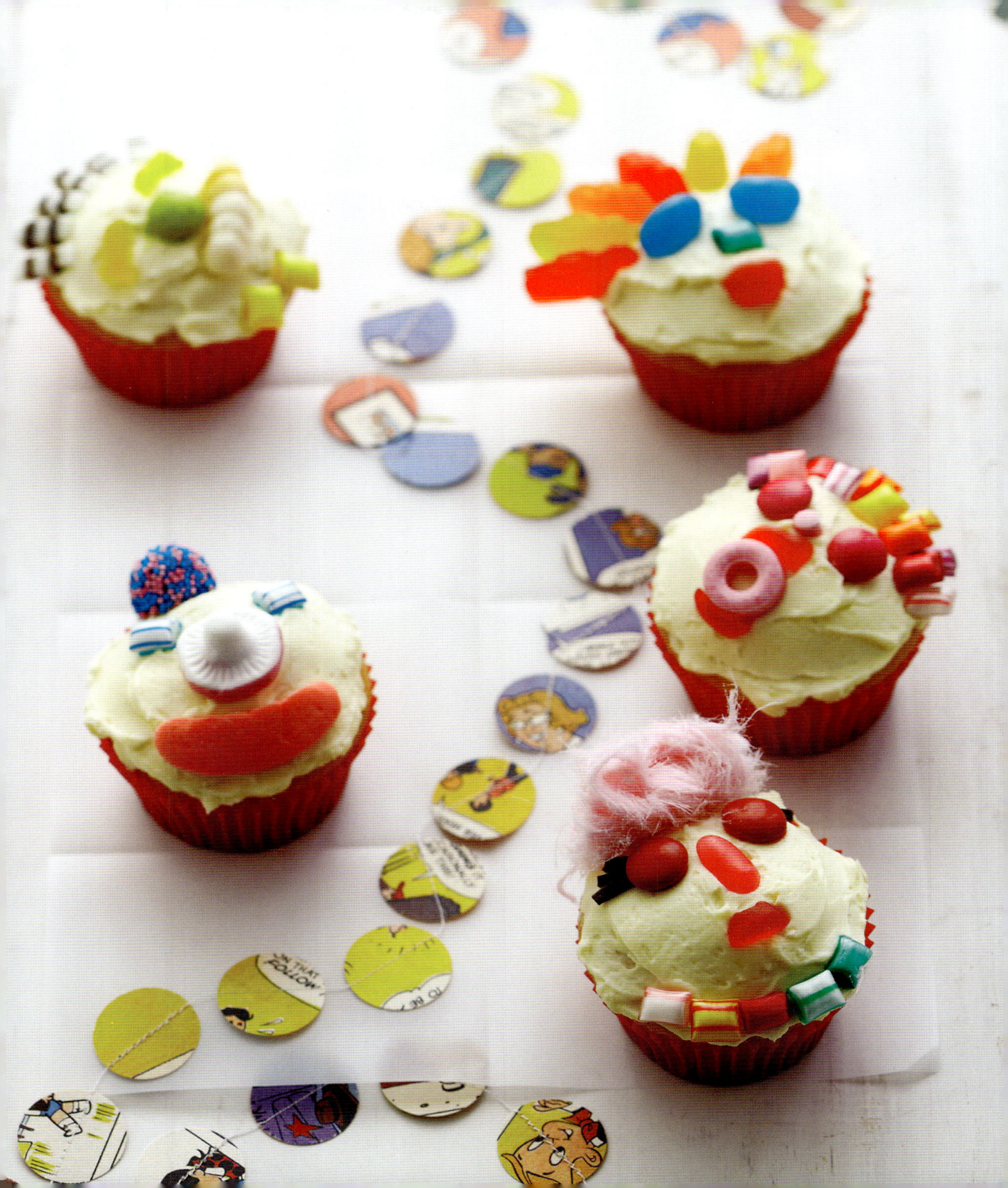

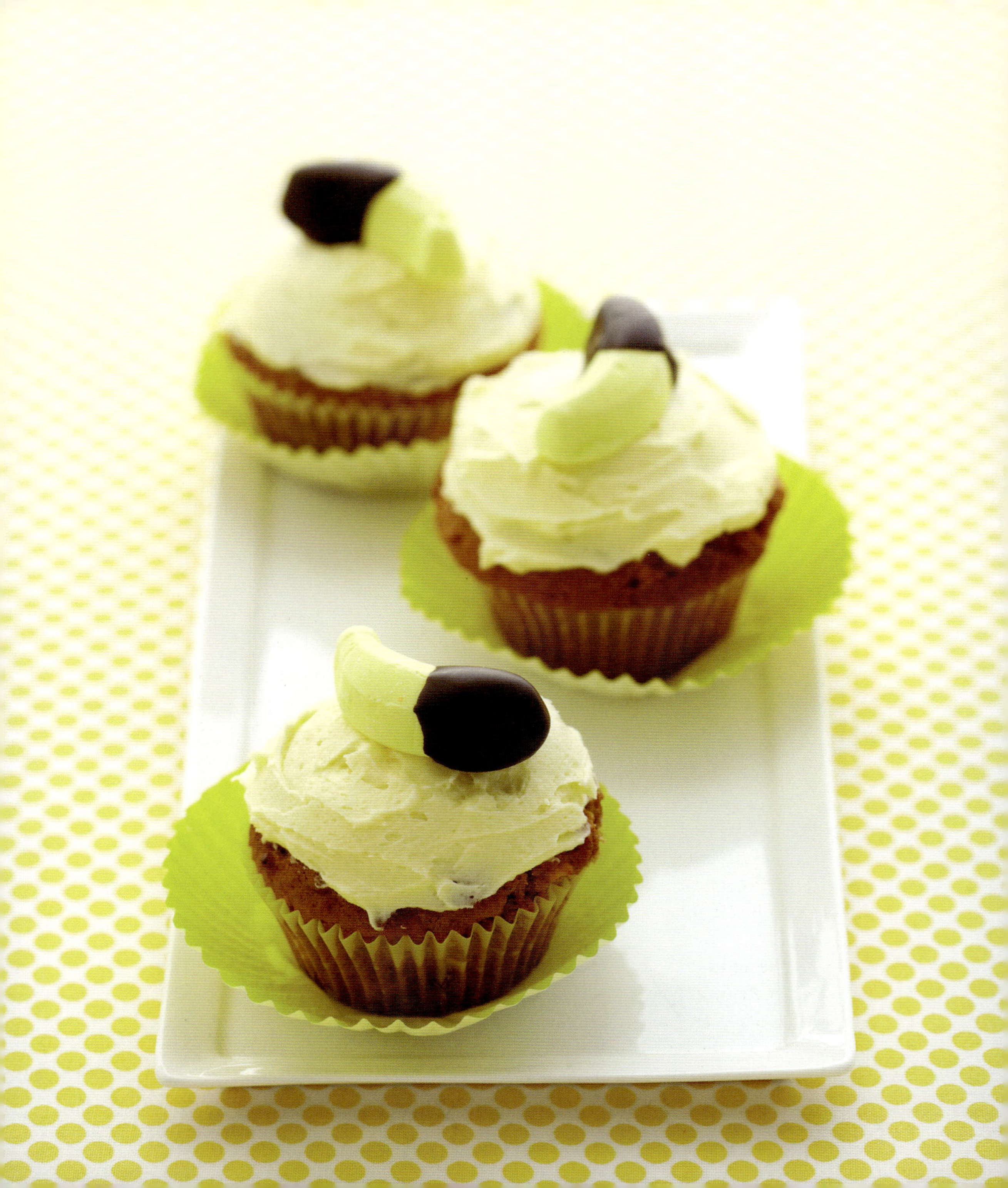

Go bananas

Preparation time: 20 minutes (+ 20 minutes standing time)
Cooking time: 25 minutes
Decorating time: 20 minutes
Makes: 12 standard cupcakes

125 g (4½ oz) unsalted butter, softened
150 g (5½ oz/¾ cup, lightly packed) soft brown sugar
2 eggs, at room temperature
225 g (8 oz/1 cup) mashed banana (see tip)
225 g (8 oz/1½ cups) self-raising flour
¼ teaspoon bicarbonate of soda
½ teaspoon ground cinnamon
85 g (3 oz/⅓ cup) sour cream
12 banana lollies
80 g (2¾ oz) dark compound chocolate, melted, cooled slightly
1 quantity vanilla buttercream (see page 123)

1 Preheat oven to 180°C (350°F/Gas 4). Line 12 standard (80 ml/2½ fl oz/⅓ cup) muffin holes with paper cases.
2 Use an electric mixer to beat the butter and sugar together in a medium bowl until creamy. Add the eggs, one at a time, beating well after each addition. Beat in the banana. Sift the flour, bicarbonate of soda and cinnamon into a medium bowl. With the mixer on low speed, add the flour and sour cream alternately in two separate batches each and mix until just combined. Divide the mixture evenly among the paper cases then smooth the tops with the back of a teaspoon.
3 Bake for 20–25 minutes, turning the tin around after 15 minutes, or until golden and a skewer inserted into the centre of a cupcake comes out clean. Allow to cool for 5 minutes in the tin before transferring to a wire rack to cool completely.
4 Meanwhile, line a tray with non-stick baking paper. Dip one end of each banana lolly into the melted chocolate and place on the tray. Set aside for 20 minutes or until set.
5 To decorate, spread the buttercream on the top of each cupcake and top with a chocolate-dipped banana.

TIPS: You will need about 2 medium ripe bananas for this recipe.

Keep iced and decorated cupcakes in an airtight container in the fridge for up to 2 days.

Marbled cupcakes

Preparation time: 30 minutes (+ cooling time)
Cooking time: 25 minutes
Decorating time: 15 minutes
Makes: 12 standard cupcakes

185 g (6½ oz/1¼ cups) plain flour
1½ teaspoons baking powder
165 g (5¾ oz/¾ cup) caster sugar
125 g (4½ oz) unsalted butter, softened
60 ml (2 fl oz/¼ cup) milk, plus 1 tablespoon, extra
3 eggs, at room temperature
1 teaspoon vanilla extract
2 tablespoons unsweetened cocoa powder, sifted
½ quantity chocolate buttercream (see page 119)
12 gumballs

TIP: Keep iced and decorated cupcakes in an airtight container in the fridge for up to 2 days. Serve at room temperature.

1 Preheat oven to 160°C (315°F/Gas 2–3). Line 12 standard (80 ml/2½ fl oz/⅓ cup) muffin holes with paper cases.
2 Sift the flour and baking powder together into a medium bowl. Add the sugar, butter, milk, eggs and vanilla. Use electric beaters to beat on low speed until combined. Increase speed to medium–high and beat for 2–3 minutes or until well combined, very smooth and the mixture is paler in colour. Place half the mixture in a clean medium bowl. Add the cocoa powder and the extra 1 tablespoon of milk to the remaining mixture and beat until well combined
3 Spoon a heaped teaspoon of the vanilla mixture into each paper case, followed by a heaped teaspoon of the chocolate mixture. Repeat until all the mixture has been used and is evenly divided among the paper cases. Swirl each cupcake with a skewer to create a marbled effect.
4 Bake for 25 minutes, turning the tin around after 15 minutes, or until golden and a skewer inserted into the centre of a cupcake comes out clean. Allow to cool for 5 minutes in the tin before transferring to a wire rack to cool completely.
5 To decorate, spread the cooled cupcakes with the buttercream and top with a gumball.

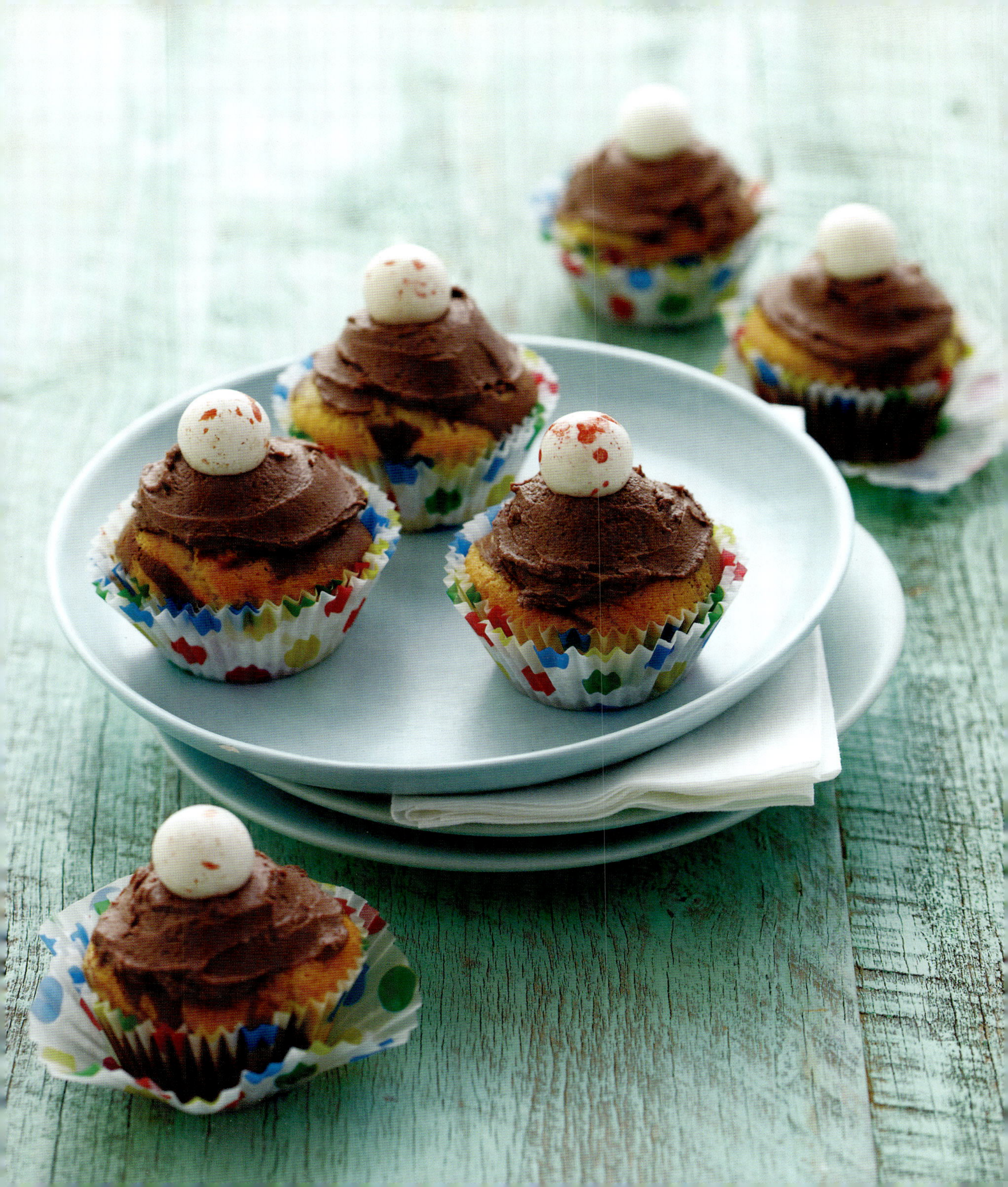

Decorate it

Hungry worms

Preparation time: 15 minutes
Cooking time: nil
Decorating time: 35 minutes
Makes: 12 standard cupcakes

>12 standard vanilla cupcakes (see page 116)
½ quantity vanilla buttercream (see page 123)
green food colouring
12 ball lollipops
licorice strap
12 candy-coated chocolate buttons
72 mini candy-coated chocolate buttons
chocolate writing icing

1 Level the tops of the cupcakes if necessary.
2 Tint the buttercream with the green food colouring to desired colour. Reserve 2 tablespoons of the buttercream and spread the remainder over the tops of the cupcakes
3 Use scissors to cut off and discard the sticks from the lollipops (see tip). Position a lollipop round, top side down, on a cupcake. Cut a strip of the licorice small enough to fit into the hole of the stick to make a stem. Repeat with the remaining cupcakes, lollipops and licorice.
4 Use a piping bag fitted with a 2 mm (1/16 in) round nozzle to pipe the reserved buttercream on the top of each lollipop to make a leaf. Position the candy-coated chocolate buttons and mini candy-coated chocolate buttons to make worms (see photo). Use the chocolate writing icing to make worm eyes.

TIPS: When cutting the sticks off the lollipops make sure you leave some of the stick protruding so that it is visible and not eaten by mistake.

Keep iced cupcakes in an airtight container in a cool place for up to 2 days. Add decorations to serve.

Writing icing is available in the baking section of the supermarket.

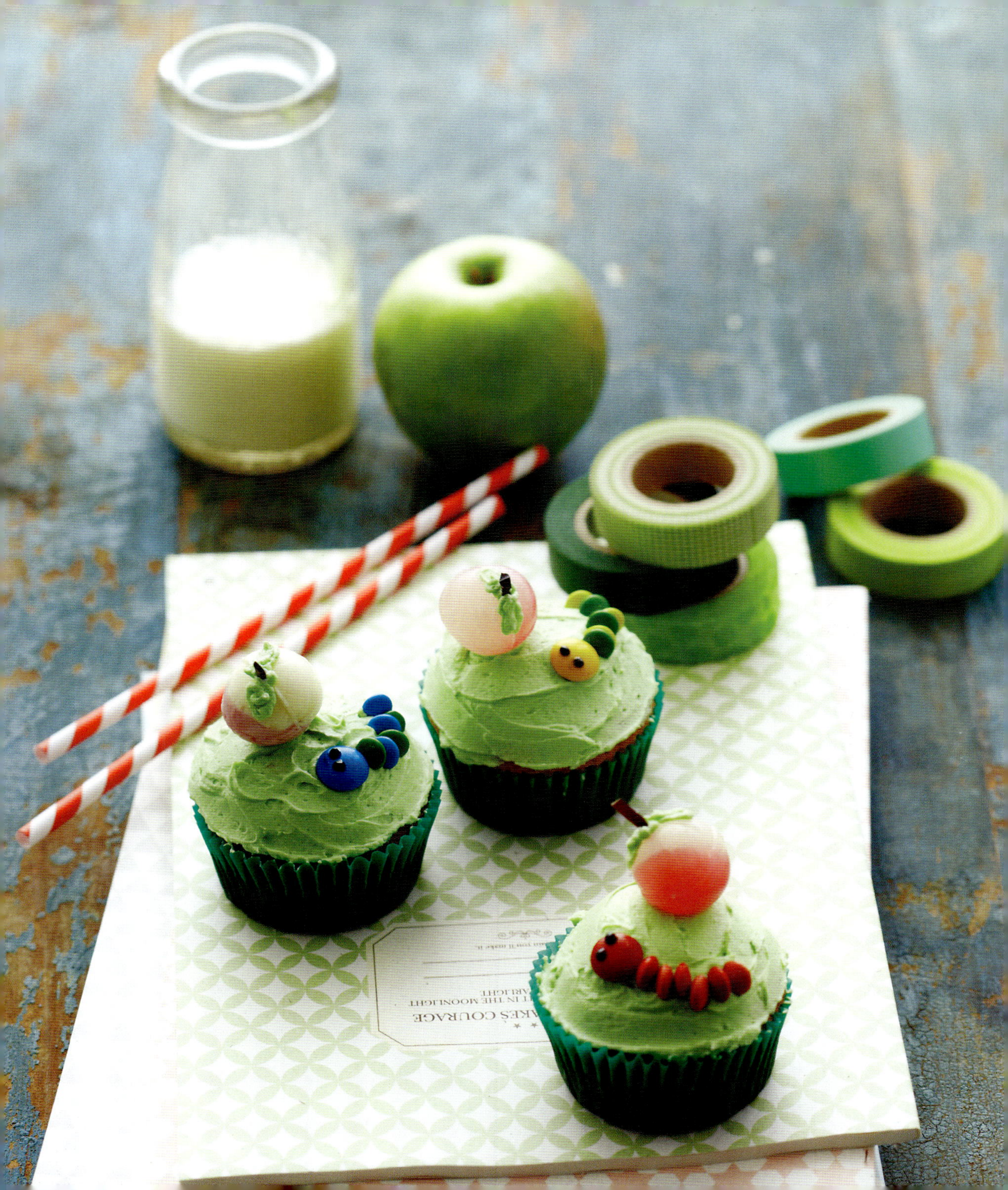

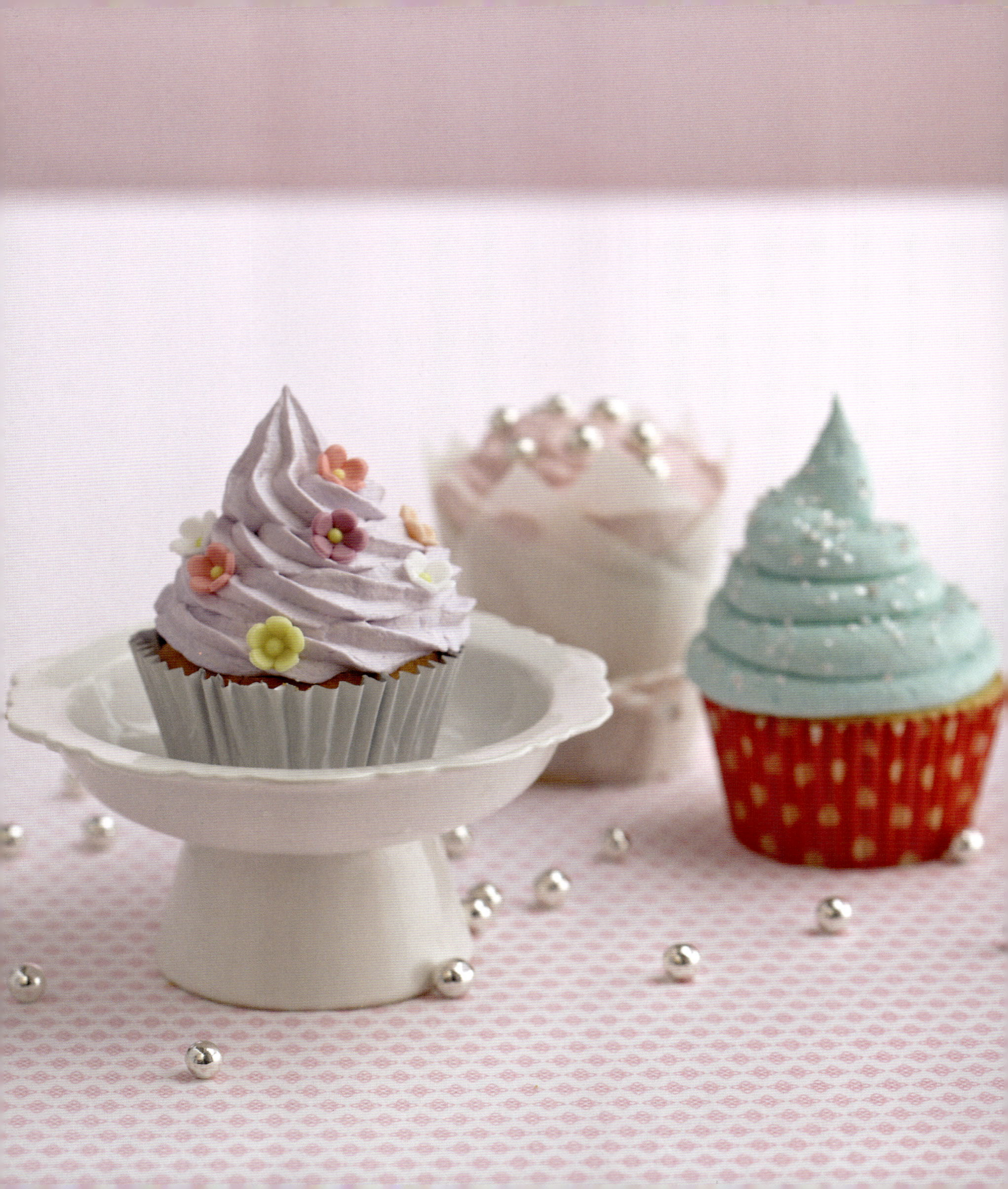

Cupcake swirls

Preparation time: 10 minutes
Cooking time: nil
Decorating time: 20 minutes
Makes: 12 standard cupcakes

> 1 quantity vanilla buttercream (see page 123)
> food colouring of your choice
> 12 standard vanilla or chocolate cupcakes (see pages 116–117)
> edible decorations and/or coloured sprinkles, to decorate

1 Tint the buttercream with the food colouring to desired colour/s. Spoon the buttercream into a piping bag fitted with a 2 cm (¾ in) star or plain nozzle.
2 Pipe a large round of the buttercream in the centre of a cupcake. Then, starting near the outside edge of the cupcake, generously pipe a swirl around and over the round of icing. Alternatively, spread the buttercream over the cupcake to cover.
3 Sprinkle with the decorations and/or sprinkles. Repeat with the remaining cupcakes, buttercream and decorations.

TIP: Keep iced and decorated cupcakes in an airtight container in the fridge for up to 2 days. Serve at room temperature.

Zebra stripes

Preparation time: 20 minutes
Cooking time: nil
Decorating time: 20 minutes
Makes: 12 standard cupcakes

> 12 standard vanilla cupcakes (see page 116)
> 55 g (2 oz/¼ cup) caster sugar
> 2 tablespoons water
> pure icing sugar, to dust
> 300 g (10½ oz) white fondant icing (fondant)
> 100 g (3½ oz) black fondant icing (fondant)

1 Level the tops of the cupcakes if necessary.

2 Put the sugar and water in a small saucepan over medium–low heat and bring to the boil, stirring until the sugar dissolves. Reduce the heat to low and gently boil for 3 minutes or until the syrup thickens slightly. Remove from the heat and cool for 15 minutes. Brush the tops of the cupcakes with a little of the cooled syrup. Reserve the remaining syrup.

3 Meanwhile, lightly dust a clean bench with icing sugar and knead the white icing until smooth and pliable. Repeat with the black icing. Divide the white and black icings into three portions each. Roll one portion of the white icing into a rectangle about 10 x 15 cm (4 x 6 in). Roll one-third of the black icing into different-sized strips. Keep the remaining white and black icings in airtight containers until required. Repeat with the remaining white and black icings.

4 To decorate, position the black icing strips onto the rolled white icing to make a zebra pattern. Use a rolling pin to roll the icing to a rectangle 20 cm x 15 cm x 5 mm deep (8 in x 6 in x ¼ in). Use a 6.5 cm (2¾ in) round cutter to cut out four rounds from the icing. Use your fingertip to neaten the edges of the discs and then position on top of a cupcake and press gently to attach. Brush the icing round with the sugar syrup. Repeat with the remaining cupcakes, icing and icing rounds, and sugar syrup.

TIPS: Using the icing in small pieces makes it easier to work with and less likely to dry out.

The black icing will mark with icing sugar as it is rolled. Remove the marks by brushing with sugar syrup — it also gives a lovely shine.

Brush the icing with the sugar syrup no more than 3 hours before serving as it may make the colours run.

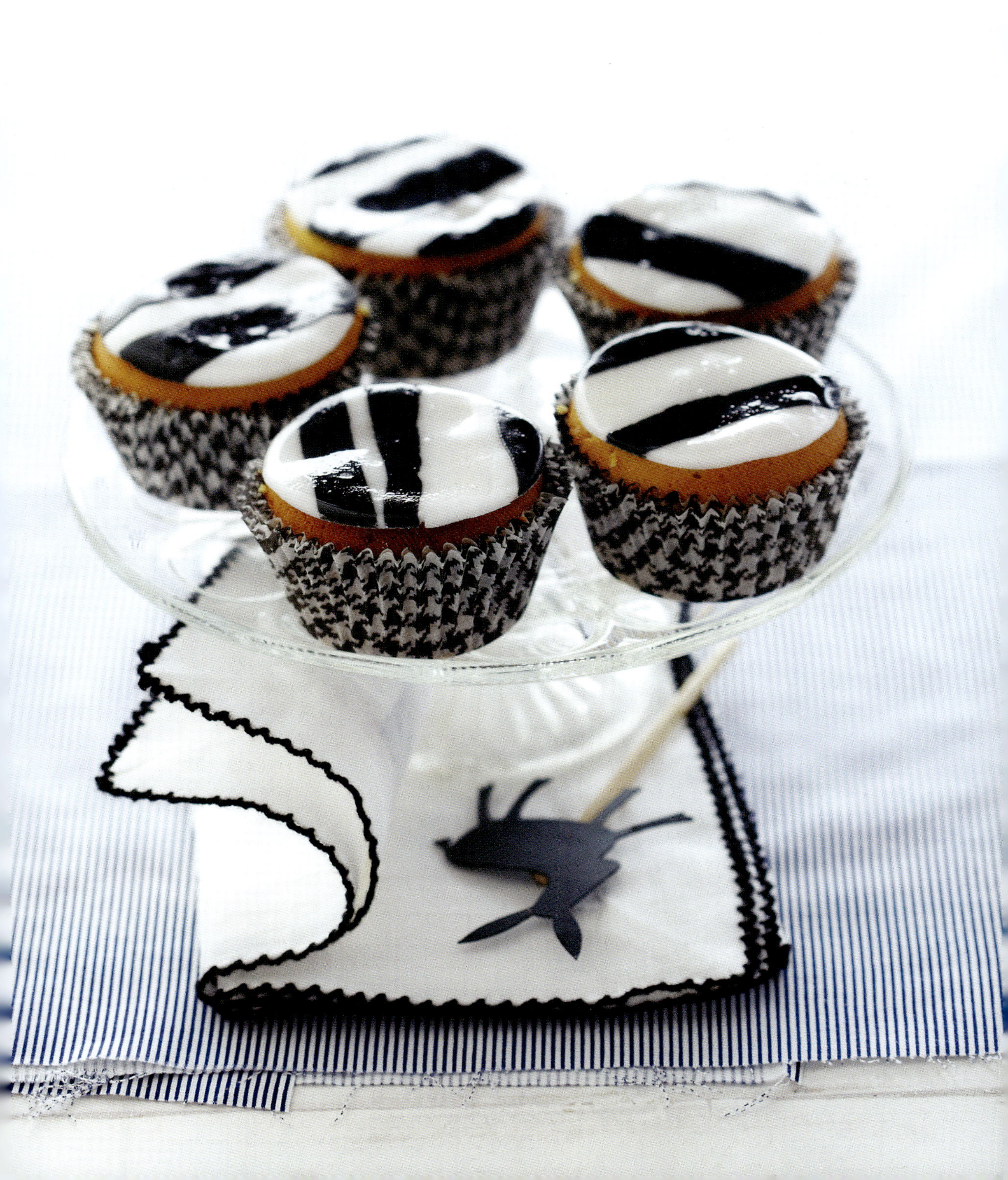

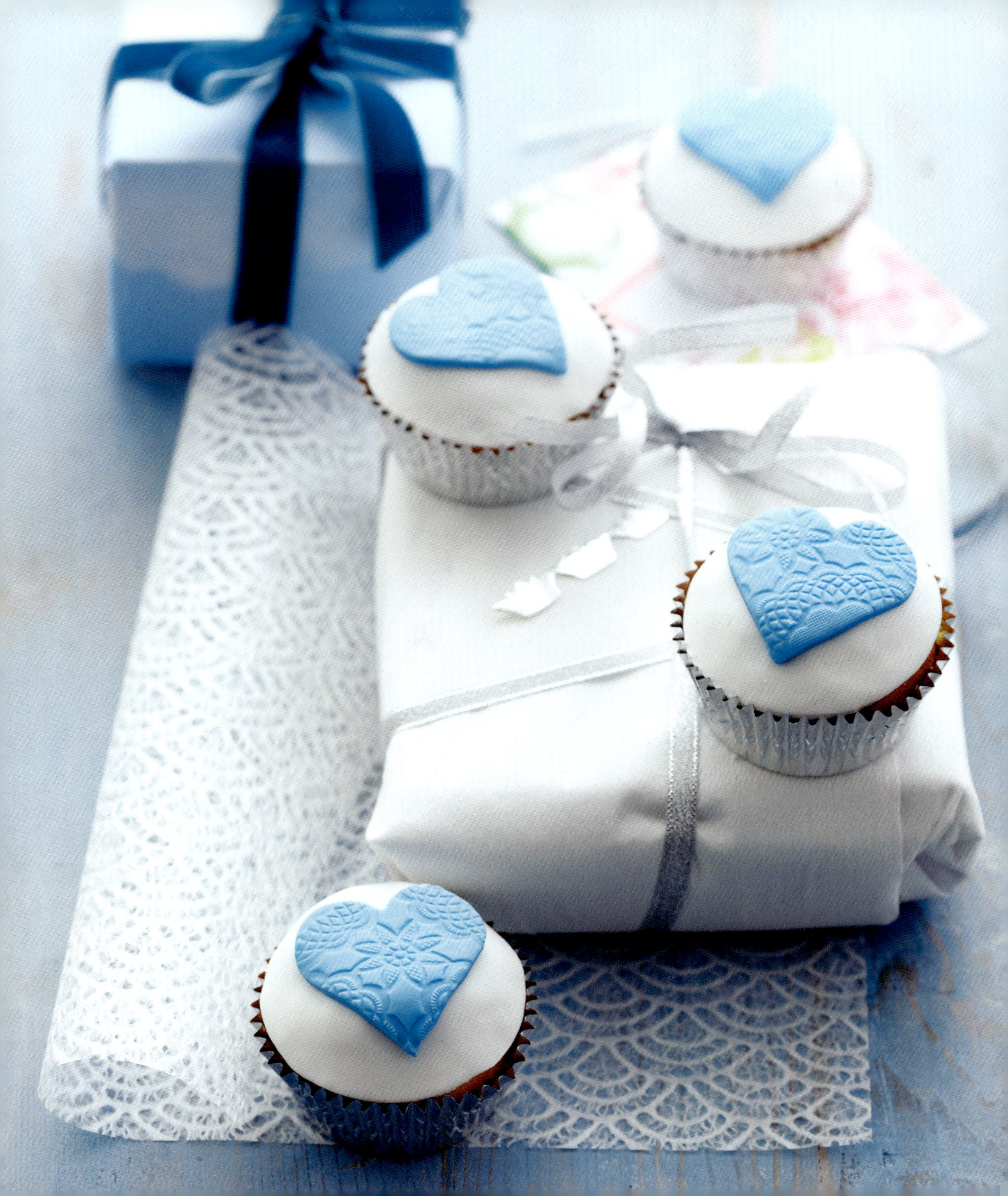

Sweet hearts

Preparation time: 5 minutes
Cooking time: nil
Decorating time: 30 minutes
Makes: 12 standard cupcakes

> 12 standard vanilla cupcakes (see page 116)
> 500 g (1 lb 2 oz) white fondant icing (fondant)
> pure icing sugar, to dust
> blue food colouring
> 50 cm (20 in) piece plastic filigree lace (see tip)

1 Level the tops of the cupcakes if necessary.
2 Divide the icing into two portions, one weighing 200 g (7 oz) and the other 300 g (10½ oz). Lightly dust a clean bench with icing sugar and knead each portion of icing until smooth and pliable. Add a little of the blue food colouring to the 200 g portion of icing. Knead, adding extra colour until tinted to desired colour. Wrap well in plastic wrap and set aside.
3 Lightly dust a clean bench with icing sugar and knead the 300 g portion of icing until smooth and pliable. Use a rolling pin to roll out to a thickness of 2 mm (1/16 in). Use a 7 cm (2¾ in) round cutter to cut 12 rounds from the icing. Use your fingertip to neaten the edge of the discs and then place on the tops of the cupcakes to cover. Press gently to attach.
4 Roll out the blue icing to a thickness of 2 mm (1/16 in). Position the piece of lace over the top. Roll firmly with a rolling pin to imprint the lace pattern onto the icing. Gently remove the lace. Use a 4.5 cm (1¾ in) heart-shaped cutter to cut out 12 hearts. Brush the base of a heart with a little water and position on the top of a cupcake. Repeat with the remaining cupcakes and hearts.

TIPS: Keep iced and decorated cupcakes in an airtight container in a cool place for up to 2 days.

You can find filigree lace at a fabric shop.

Dotty cakes

Preparation: 10 minutes
Cooking time: nil
Decorating time: 20 minutes
Makes: 24 mini cupcakes

½ quantity vanilla buttercream (see page 123)
blue, pink and yellow food colouring
24 mini vanilla cupcakes (see page 116)
2 teaspoons coloured sprinkles

TIP: These cupcakes are best decorated just before serving.

1 Tint 1 cup of the buttercream with the blue food colouring to desired colour. Tint two-thirds of the remaining buttercream with the pink food colouring to desired colour. Tint the remaining buttercream with the yellow food colouring to desired colour.
2 Use a piping bag fitted with a 1 cm (½ in) round nozzle to pipe the blue buttercream in a round on the top of each cupcake. Use a piping bag fitted with a 0.7 cm (5/16 in) round nozzle to pipe the pink icing in a round on top of the blue icing. Use a piping bag fitted with a 0.5 cm (¼ in) round nozzle to pipe a yellow round on top of the pink icing. Top with the coloured sprinkles.

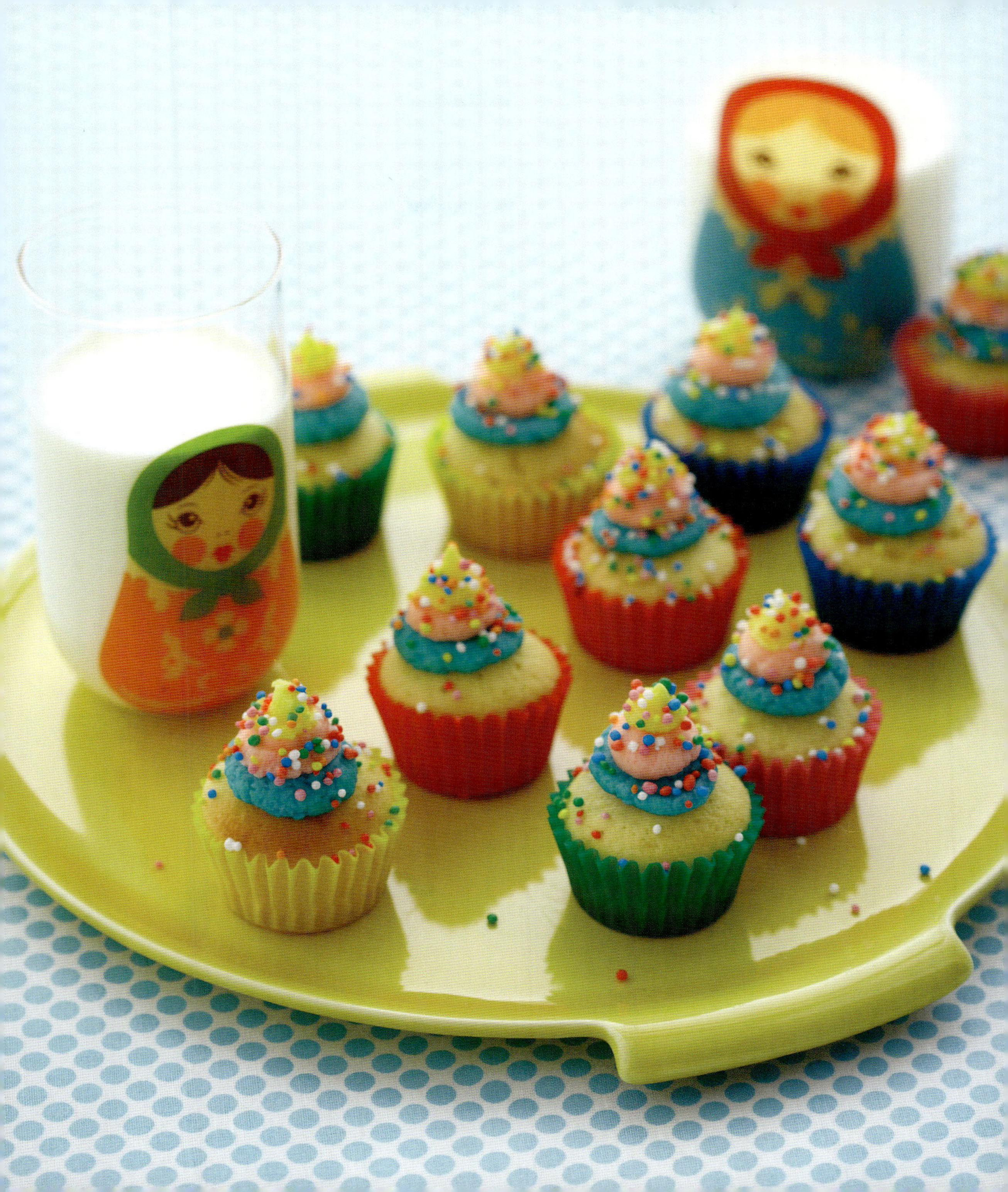

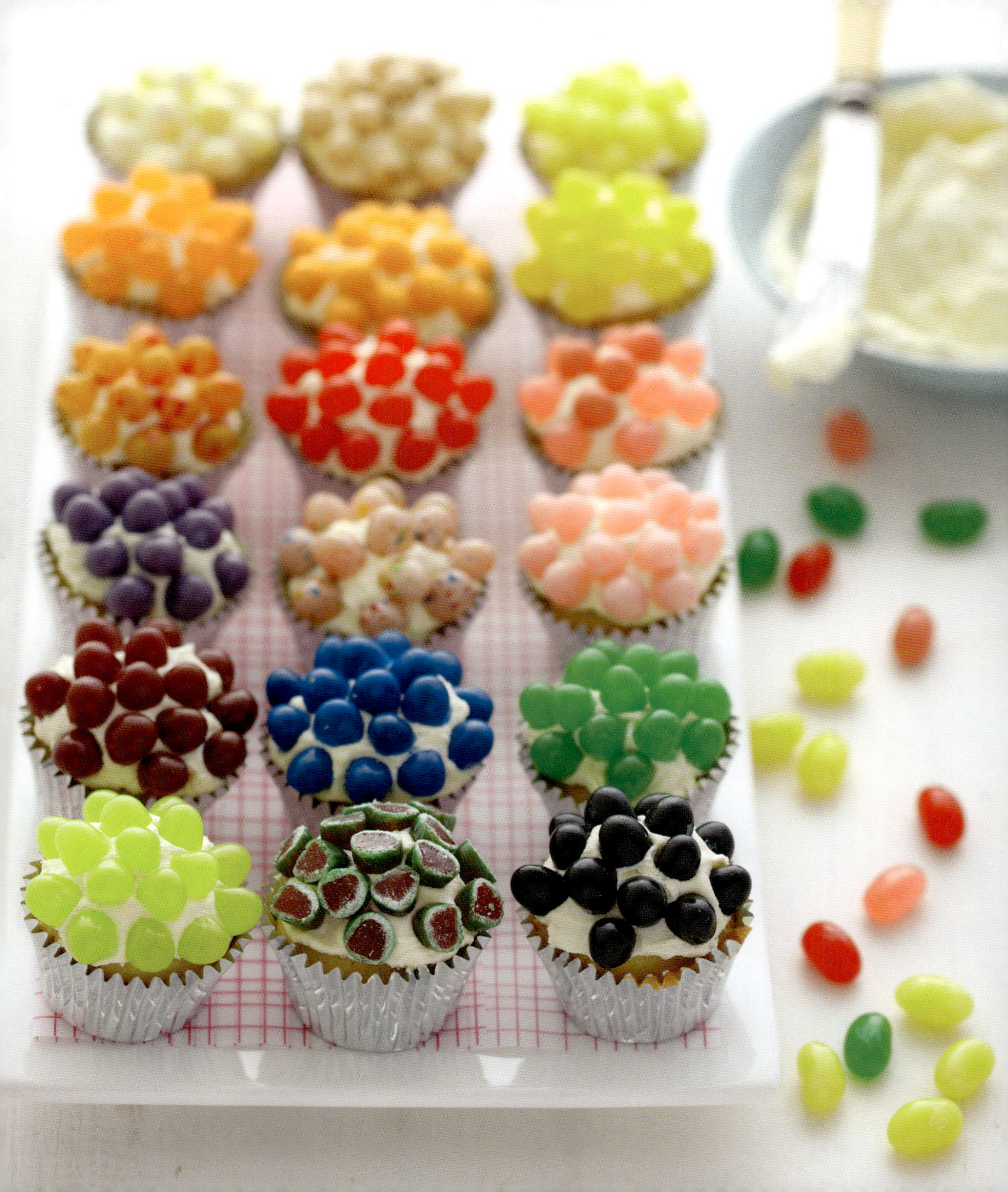

Jumping jelly beans

Preparation time: 10 minutes
Cooking time: nil
Decorating time: 1 hour
Makes: 24 mini cupcakes

½ quantity vanilla buttercream (see page 123)
food colourings, as desired (optional)
24 mini vanilla cupcakes (see page 116)
240 g (8¾ oz) mini jelly beans (you will need 6–8 similar coloured beans for each cake)

1 Tint the buttercream with the food colouring/s, if using, to desired colour and spread over the cupcakes.
2 Cut the jelly beans in half crossways. Position the jelly bean halves, cut side down, on top of the cupcakes. If the colours are interesting, you might like to place some cut side up.

TIP: Keep iced and decorated cupcakes in an airtight container in the fridge for up to 2 days. Serve at room temperature.

Stampin' cupcakes

Preparation time: 5 minutes
Cooking time: nil
Decorating time: 35 minutes
Makes: 6 large cupcakes

> 6 large vanilla or chocolate cupcakes (see pages 116–117)
> pure icing sugar, to dust
> 500 g (1 lb 2 oz) white fondant icing (fondant)
> liquid food colouring of your choice
> 2 tablespoons apricot jam, warmed, sieved

1 Level the tops of the cupcakes if necessary.
2 Lightly dust a clean bench with icing sugar and knead the icing until smooth and pliable. Use a rolling pin to roll out the icing to a thickness of 5 mm (¼ in).
3 Place a 5 cm (2 in) square piece of chux cloth or a double layer of muslin (cheesecloth) over a small plate with a lip. Pour a small amount of food colouring onto the cloth (just enough to soak it). Place four layers of paper towel on another plate (this will be your blotter).
4 Press a stamp (see tip) onto the ink to coat. Blot gently on the paper towel and check that the sides are clean (if necessary, clean with cotton buds). Press gently onto the top left-hand side of the rolled icing. Continue the process, adding extra food colouring as necessary and stamping the design close together in rows, to cover the whole surface of the icing. Allow to stand for 20 minutes or until the food colouring is dry.
5 Use a 9 cm (3½ in) round cutter to cut out six rounds from the icing. Brush a cupcake top with a little of the warmed jam. Use your fingertip to neaten the edge of a round and then place on the top of a cupcake to cover. Repeat with the remaining cupcakes, jam and icing rounds.

TIPS: We used a 6 cm (2½ in) rubber car stamp from a craft shop to decorate our cupcakes. You can use any design — just make sure the design is simple and bold for best results (the design will smudge if there is too much detail).

Keep iced cupcakes in an airtight container in a cool place for up to 2 days.

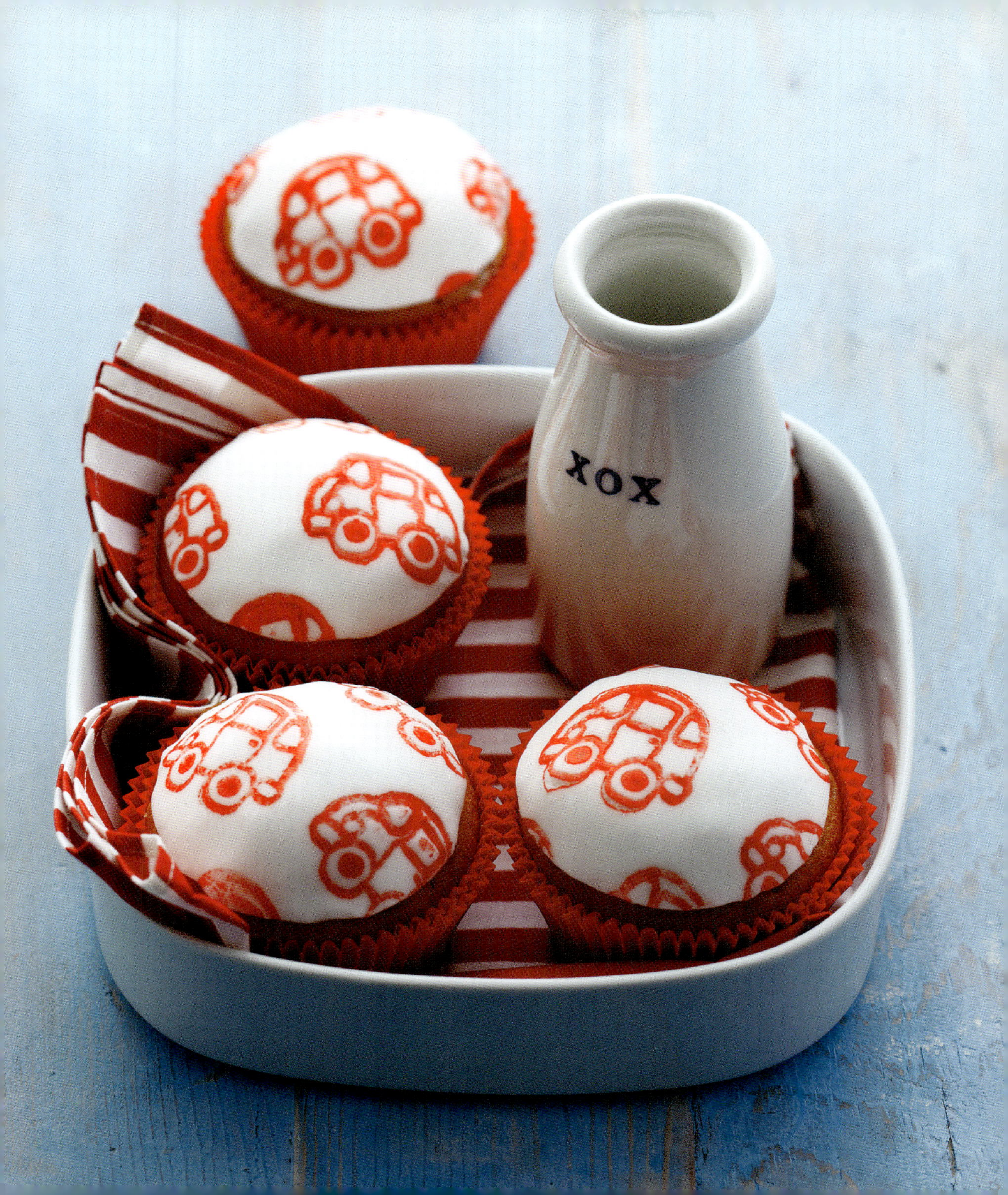
XOX

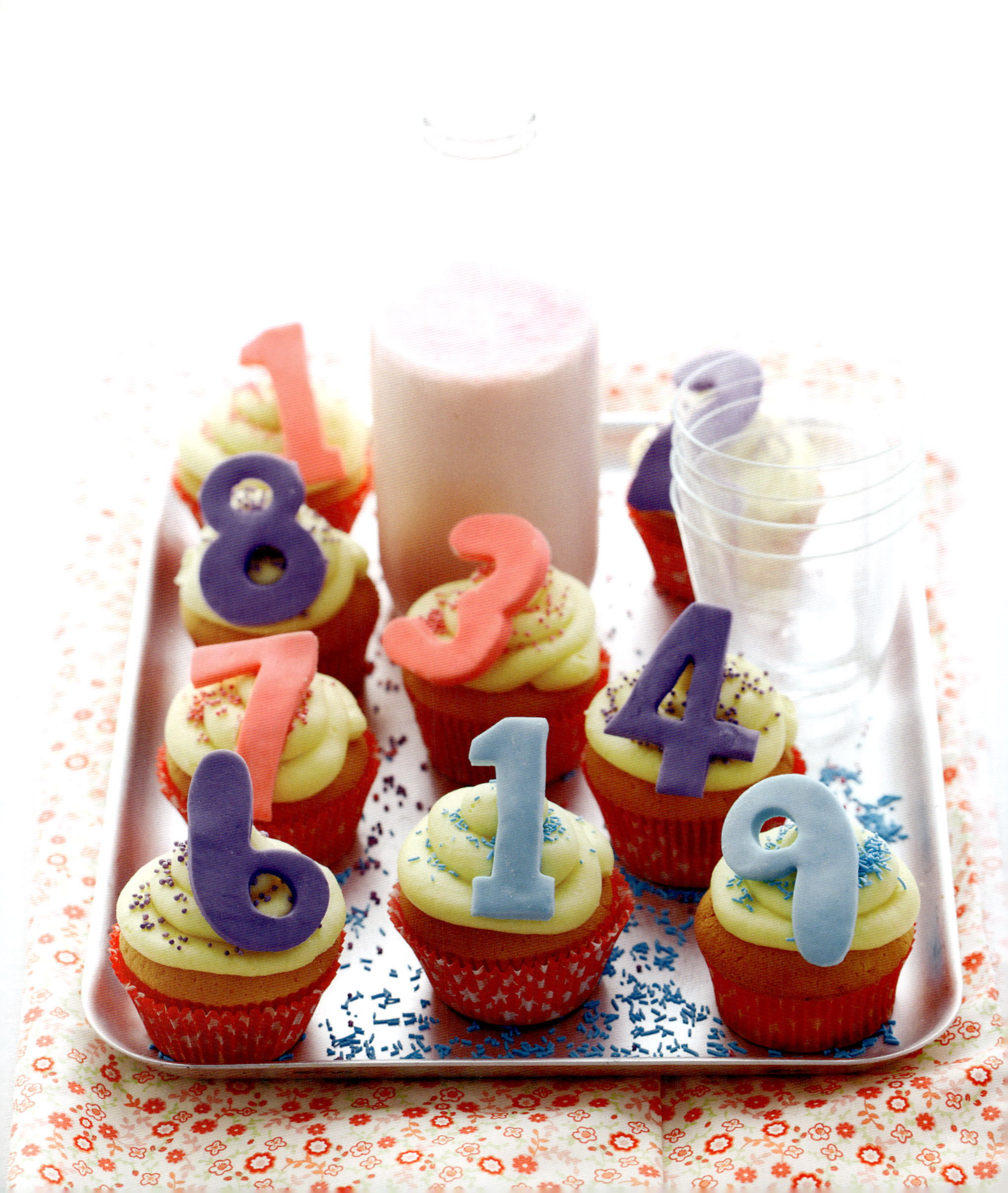

Your number's up

Preparation time: 30 minutes (+ 1 hour setting time + overnight drying time)
Cooking time: nil
Decorating time: 45 minutes
Makes: 12 standard cupcakes

> 12 standard vanilla cupcakes (see page 116)
> pure icing sugar, to dust
> 250 g (9 oz) white fondant icing (fondant)
> food colourings of your choice
> 300 g (10½ oz) white chocolate, finely chopped
> 150 ml (5 fl oz) pouring (whipping) cream
> ½ quantity vanilla buttercream (see page 123)
> coloured sprinkles, to decorate

1 Level the tops of the cupcakes if necessary.

2 Line a tray with baking paper. Lightly dust a clean bench with icing sugar and knead the icing until smooth and pliable. Divide into portions and tint with the food colourings to desired colour. Use a rolling pin to roll out the icing to a thickness of 5 mm (¼ in). Use number cutters to cut out 12 numbers and place on the prepared tray. Cover and set aside at room temperature to dry overnight, turning once after a few hours.

3 Put the chocolate in a medium heatproof bowl. Heat the cream in a small saucepan until it just comes to the boil and pour over the chocolate. Stand for 1 minute, then stir until the chocolate melts and the mixture is smooth. Set aside to cool for 15–20 minutes. Fold the cold white chocolate mixture gently into the buttercream. If the mixture is not at piping consistency set aside until it thickens slightly. Use a piping bag fitted with a 1 cm (½ in) plain nozzle to pipe the buttercream over the top of each cupcake.

4 Sprinkle the cupcakes with the coloured sprinkles and place an icing number on top of each. Set aside at room temperature for 30–60 minutes or until the icing sets.

TIPS: The numbers can be made several weeks ahead. Store in an airtight container.

Keep iced and decorated cupcakes in an airtight container in the fridge for up to 2 days. Serve at room temperature.

All buttoned up

Preparation time: 10 minutes (+ 2 hours standing time)
Cooking time: nil
Decorating time: 1 hour
Makes: 12 standard cupcakes

12 standard vanilla cupcakes (see page 116)
pure icing sugar, to dust
food colouring of your choice
600 g (1 lb 5 oz) white fondant icing (fondant)
85 g (3 oz/¼ cup) apricot jam, warmed, sieved

TIP: Keep iced and decorated cupcakes in an airtight container in a cool place for up to 2 days.

1 Level the tops of the cupcakes if necessary.
2 Lightly dust a clean bench with icing sugar and knead the icing until smooth and pliable. Use the food colouring to tint 200 g (7 oz) of the icing to desired colour or colours.
3 Put the remaining uncoloured icing in a zip-lock bag and seal. Set aside. Lightly dust a clean work bench with a little icing sugar and use a rolling pin to roll out the coloured icing to 3 mm (⅛ in) thick. Use a selection of small (1.5–3 cm/⅝–1¼ in) round and flower-shaped cutters to cut out shapes from the icing, re-rolling as necessary. Use small round cutters to mark a rim on the larger circles. Use the flat end of a wooden skewer to mark button holes and flower centres on the shapes as shown. Place the shapes on a wire rack or a baking tray lined with baking paper and set aside for 2 hours or until firm.
4 Meanwhile, lightly dust the bench again with a little icing sugar and use the rolling pin to roll out the reserved uncoloured icing to 5 mm (¼ in) thick. Use a 7 cm (2¾ in) round cutter to cut out 12 rounds, re-rolling as necessary. Brush a cupcake top with a little of the warmed jam. Use your fingertip to neaten the edge of a disc and then place on the top of a cupcake to cover. Repeat with the remaining cupcakes, jam and icing discs. Set aside with the button decorations to firm.
5 Dab a little water on the base of the buttons and flowers and attach to the iced cupcakes as desired.

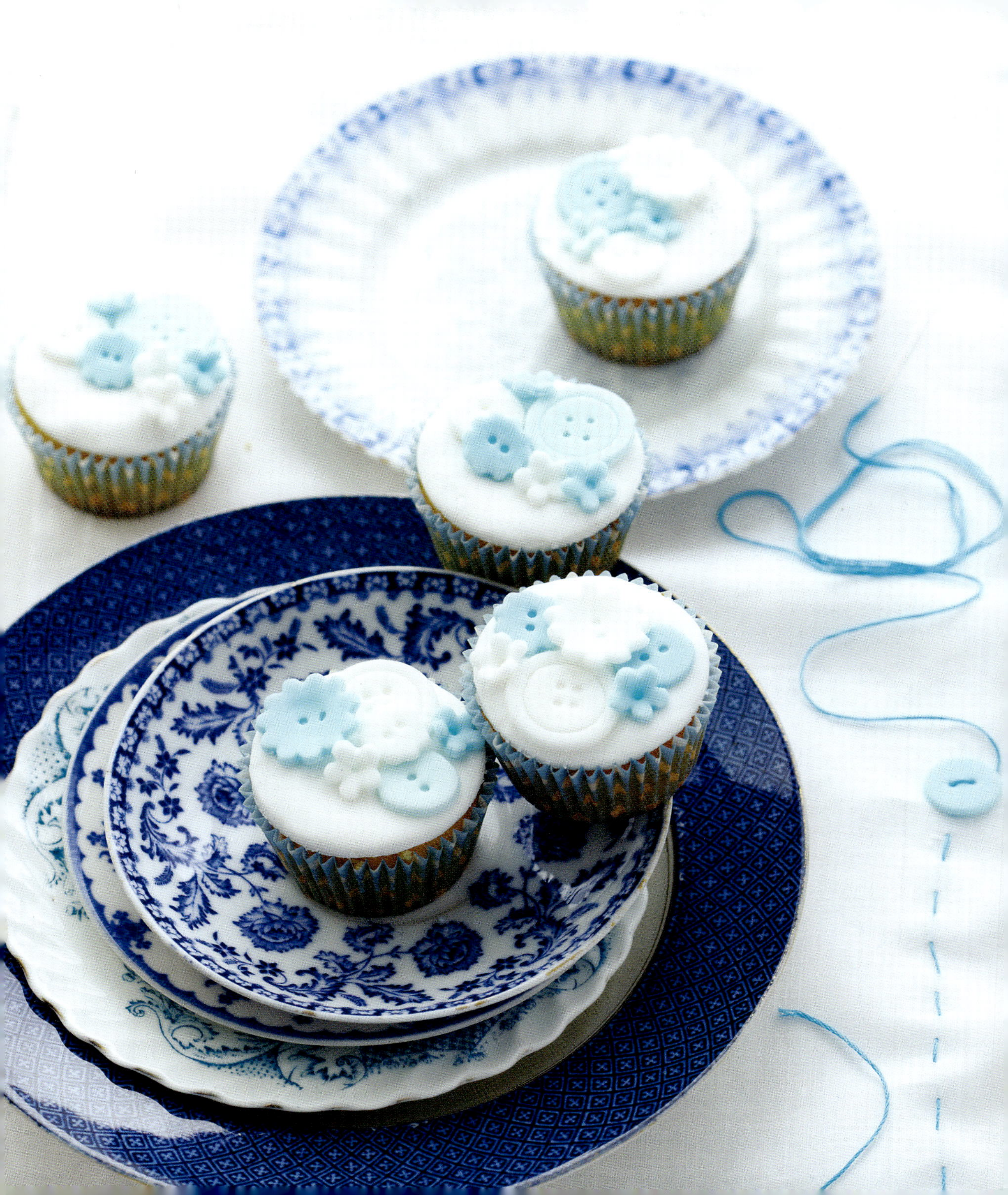

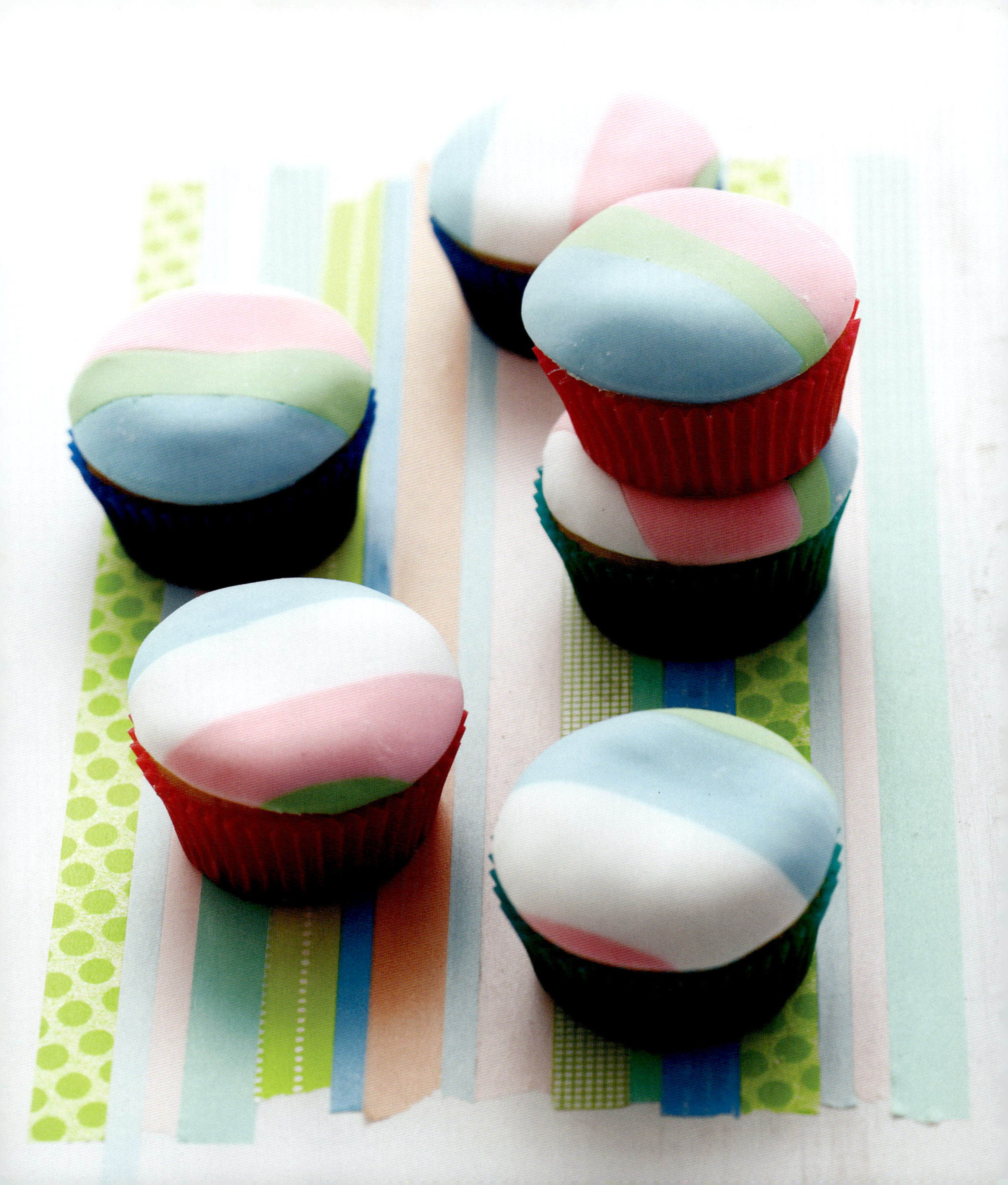

Stripe-a-luscious

Preparation time: 10 minutes
Cooking time: nil
Decorating time: 35 minutes
Makes: 12 standard cupcakes

12 standard vanilla cupcakes (see page 116)
85 g (3 oz/¼ cup) apricot jam, warmed, sieved
pure icing sugar, to dust
500 g (1 lb 2 oz) white fondant icing (fondant)
assorted food colourings

1 Level the tops of the cupcakes if necessary. Brush the tops of the cakes lightly with the apricot jam.

2 Lightly dust a clean bench with icing sugar and knead the icing until smooth and pliable. Divide into four portions. Tint three portions different colours using the food colouring. Divide each portion of white and coloured icings in half. Roll each piece into a sausage shape about 1 cm (½ in) thick. Brush the edges of the rolls with a little water and join the colours together into a square shape.

3 Use a rolling pin to roll out the icing square until 3 mm (⅛ in) thick. Use a 7 cm (2¾ in) round cutter to cut out 12 rounds from the icing. Place the icing rounds on top of the cupcakes and smooth with your fingers, pressing gently to attach.

TIPS: You can vary the icing colours used depending on the party theme.

Keep iced cupcakes in an airtight container in a cool place for up to 2 days.

Make it sparkle

Preparation time: 10 minutes (+ 1 hour setting time)
Cooking time: nil
Decorating time: 45 minutes
Makes: 12 standard cupcakes

>12 standard vanilla cupcakes (see page 116)
>85 g (3 oz/¼ cup) apricot jam, warmed, sieved
>pure icing sugar, to dust
>500 g (1 lb 2 oz) white fondant icing (fondant)
>1 quantity royal icing (see page 119)
>assorted coloured cachous, to decorate

1 Level the tops of the cupcakes if necessary. Brush the tops of the cakes lightly with the apricot jam.
2 Lightly dust a clean bench with icing sugar and knead the icing until smooth and pliable. Use a rolling pin to roll out the icing until 3 mm (⅛ in) thick. Use a 7 cm (2¾ in) round cutter to cut out rounds from the icing. Place the icing rounds on top of the cupcakes and smooth with your fingers.
3 Put the royal icing in a piping bag, snip off a small end and pipe shapes over the tops of the cupcakes, such as hearts, snowflakes, stars, initials or Christmas trees. Decorate with cachous and set aside at room temperature for 1 hour or until the icing sets.

TIP: Keep iced and decorated cupcakes in an airtight container in the fridge for up to 2 days. Serve at room temperature.

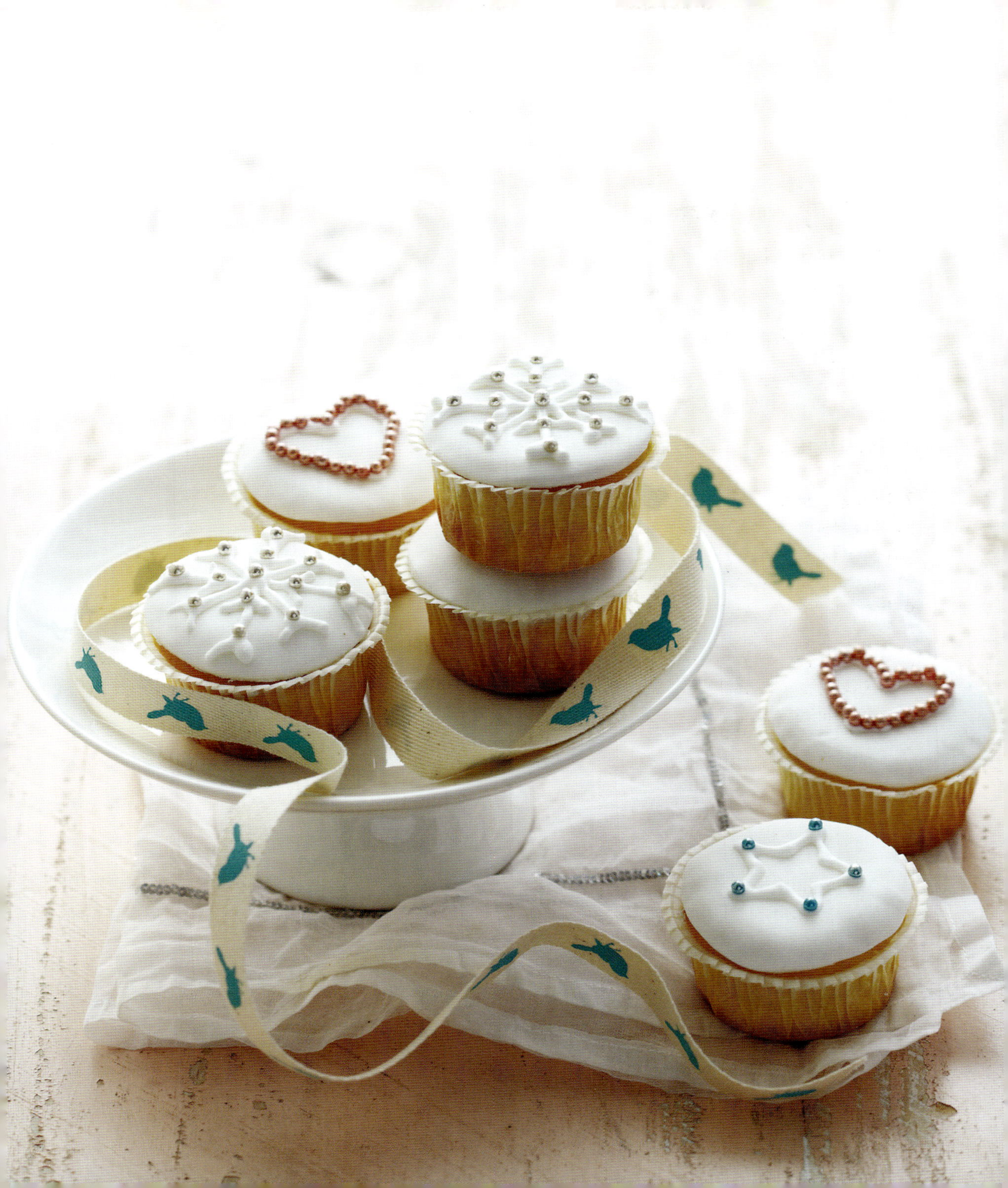

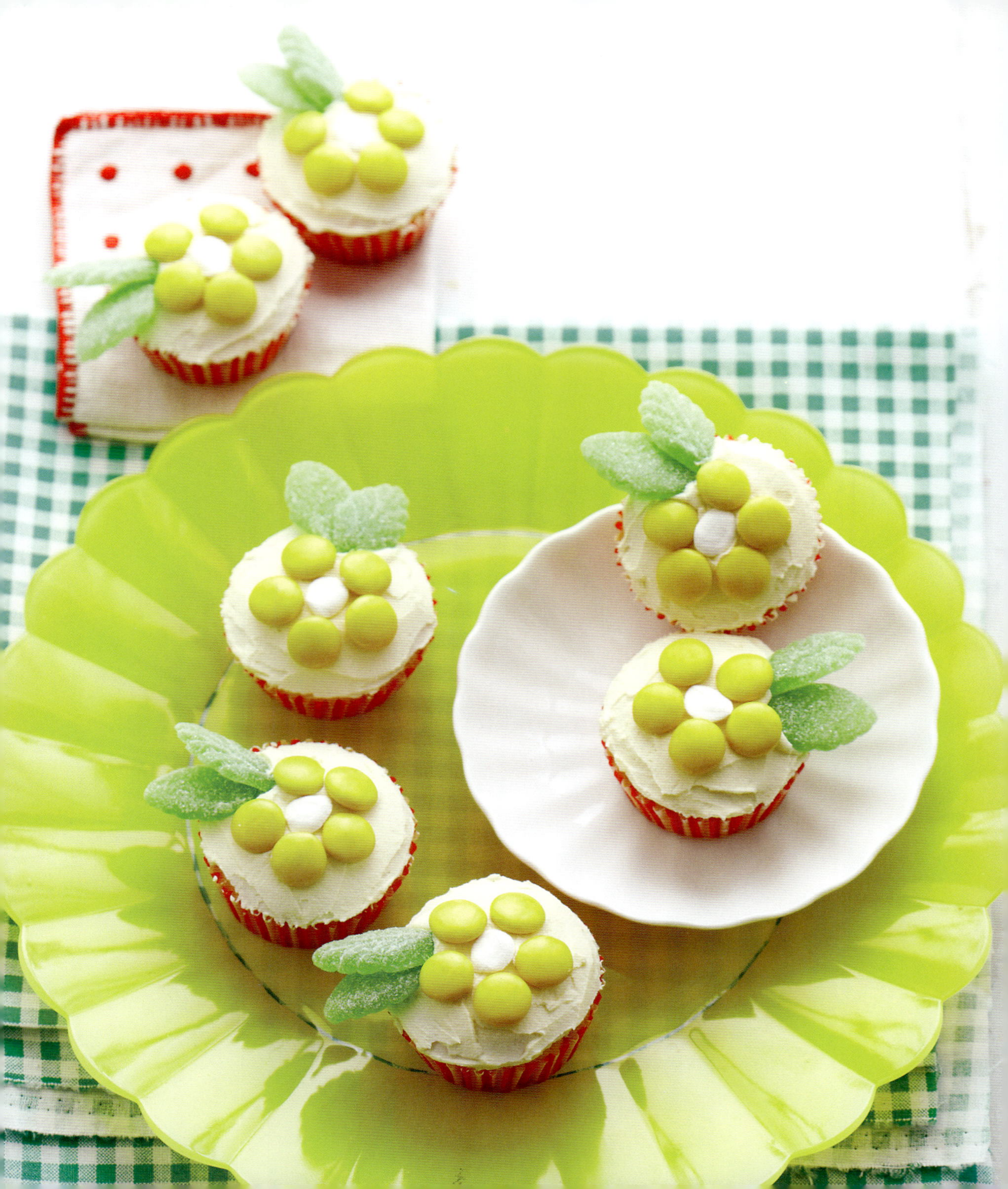

Daisy cakes

Preparation time: 10 minutes
Cooking time: nil
Decorating time: 40 minutes
Makes: 24 patty pan cupcakes

24 vanilla patty pan cupcakes (see page 116)
½ quantity vanilla buttercream (see page 119)
yellow food colouring
12 white mini marshmallows, halved
12 mint leaf lollies, halved horizontally
360 g (12¾ oz) candy-coated chocolate buttons

TIP: Keep iced and decorated cupcakes in an airtight container in a cool place for up to 2 days.

1 Level the tops of the cupcakes if necessary.
2 Tint the buttercream with the yellow food colouring to desired colour and spread over the cupcakes. Place a marshmallow half in the centre of each cupcake and place five candy-coated chocolate buttons around the marshmallow to form petals. Cut the mint leaf lollies in half through the centre. Place two pieces of mint leaves at the edge of each flower as leaves.

Decadent

Flourless chocolate cakes

Preparation time: 35 minutes
Cooking time: 40 minutes
Decorating time: 10 minutes
Makes: 12 standard cupcakes

120 g (4¼ oz) unsalted butter, diced
60 ml (2 fl oz/¼ cup) milk
180 g (6¼ oz) dark chocolate, chopped
220 g (7¾ oz/1 cup, firmly packed) soft brown sugar
110 g (3¾ oz/1 cup) hazelnut meal
3 eggs, at room temperature, separated
½ quantity dark chocolate ganache (see page 120)
2 tablespoons roasted hazelnuts, coarsely chopped

1 Preheat oven to 180°C (350°F/Gas 4). Line 12 standard (80 ml/2½ fl oz/⅓ cup) muffin holes with paper cases.
2 Put the butter, milk, chocolate and brown sugar in a small saucepan and stir over low heat until combined. Transfer to a large bowl. Cool for 10 minutes. Stir in the hazelnut meal and egg yolks.
3 Put the egg whites in a medium clean, dry bowl and use electric beaters to whisk until soft peaks form. Use a large metal spoon to stir one-third of the egg whites into the chocolate mixture to loosen it a little. Then, very gently and gradually, fold the remaining egg whites into the chocolate mixture. Divide the mixture among the paper cases.
4 Bake for 40 minutes, turning the tin around after 20 minutes, or until just firm when gently pressed. Allow to cool for 5 minutes in the tin before transferring to a wire rack to cool completely.
5 To decorate, spread the cupcakes with the ganache and sprinkle with the hazelnuts.

> **TIP:** Keep iced and decorated cupcakes in an airtight container in the fridge for up to 2 days. Serve at room temperature.

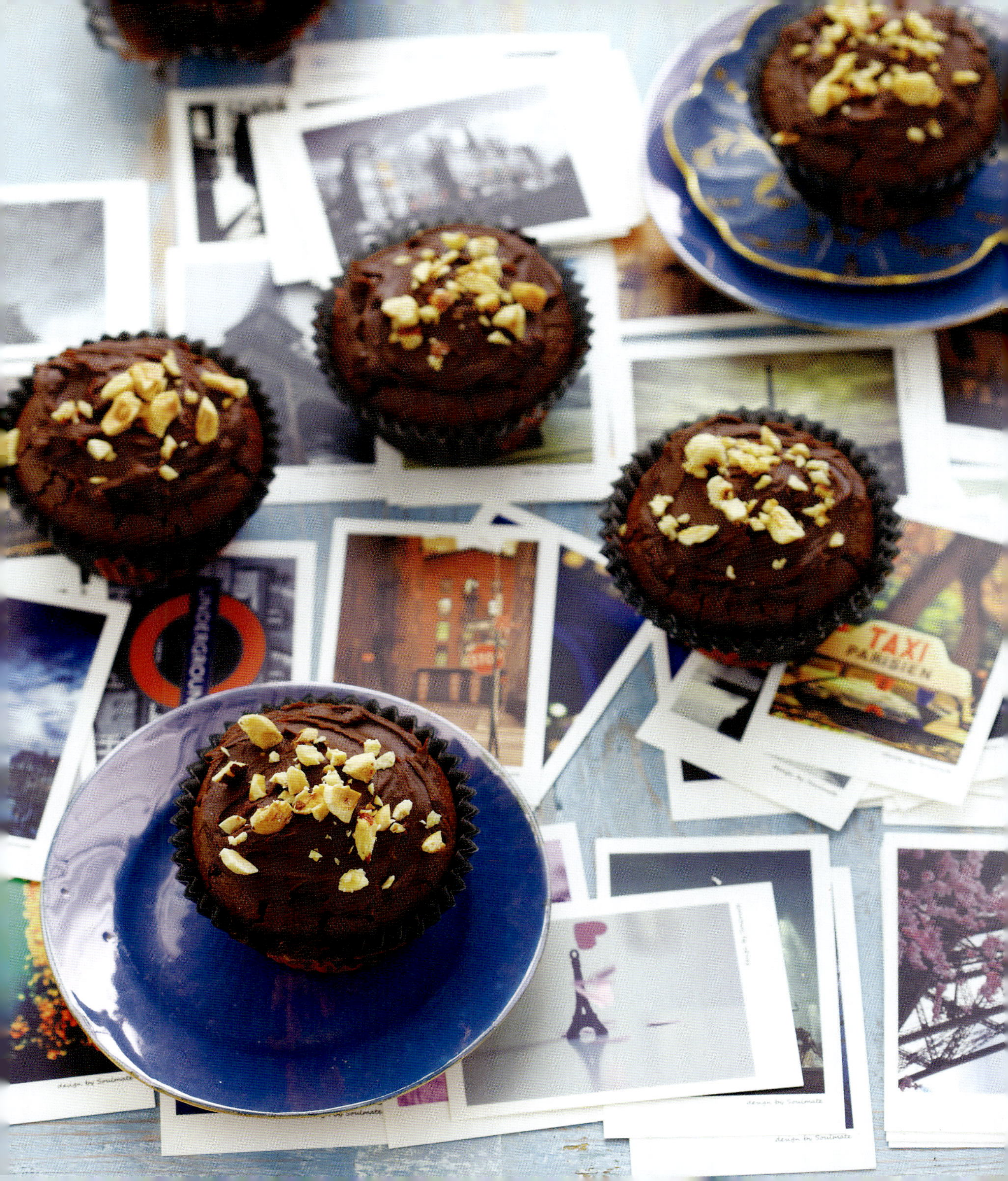
TAXI
PARISIEN

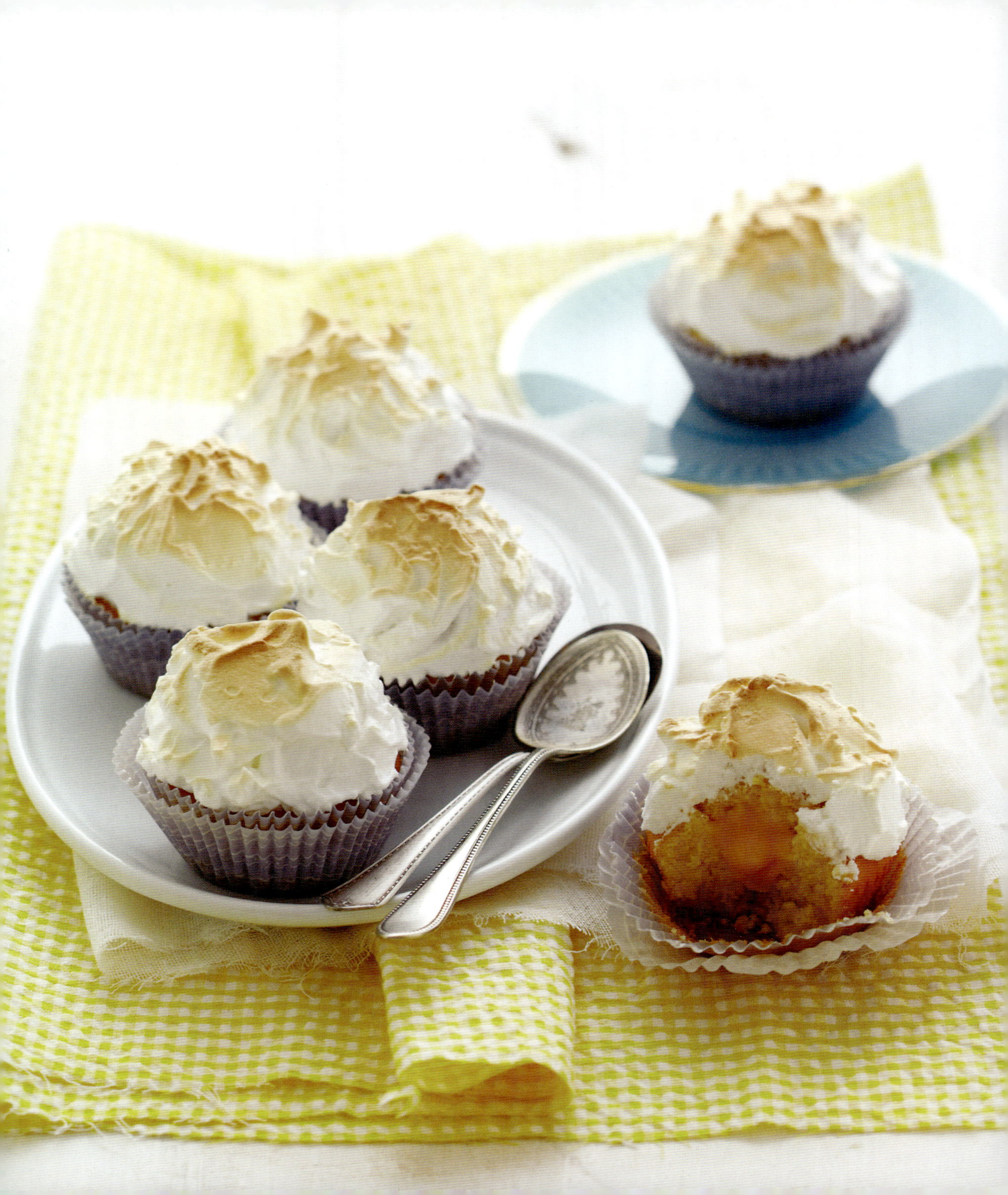

Lemon meringue cupcakes

Preparation time: 25 minutes (+ 1 hour chilling time + 15 minutes cooling time)
Cooking time: 8 minutes
Makes: 12 standard cupcakes

12 standard lemon cupcakes (see pages 116–117)

Lemon curd
2 egg yolks
2 tablespoons caster sugar
1 lemon, zest finely grated, juice strained
 (you will need 60 ml/2 fl oz/¼ cup lemon juice)
65 g (2½ oz) unsalted butter, diced

Meringue
2 egg whites, at room temperature
110 g (3¾ oz/½ cup) caster sugar

TIP: Keep cupcakes in an airtight container in the fridge for up to 2 days. Serve at room temperature.

1 To make the lemon curd, put the egg yolks, sugar, lemon zest and juice in a medium heatproof bowl and use a balloon whisk to combine. Add the butter and place over a saucepan of simmering water, making sure the base of the bowl doesn't touch the water. Cook for 4 minutes, stirring constantly with a wooden spoon, until thick. Remove from the heat. Strain through a coarse sieve into a bowl, cover the surface with plastic wrap and refrigerate for 1 hour or until chilled.
2 Use a small, sharp pointed knife to cut a 3 cm (1¼ in) hole about 3 cm (1¼ in) deep in the top of each cupcake. Reserve the pieces you have removed and trim to 1 cm (½ in) deep. Use a piping bag with the tip cut off to pipe the lemon curd into the cupcake holes. Replace the cut-out pieces.
3 Preheat grill (broiler) to high. To make the meringue, put the egg whites in a large clean, dry bowl and beat with electric beaters until soft peaks form. Continue beating, gradually adding the sugar, a spoonful at a time, until thick and glossy. Spoon the meringue on top of the cupcakes and use a palette knife to create waves of meringue or pointy spikes. Put six of the cupcakes on a baking tray and place under the grill on the centre rack of the oven for 30 seconds. Turn the tray and grill for another 30 seconds, watching closely, or until the meringue is golden. Repeat with the remaining cupcakes.
4 Set aside until the meringue is cool then serve.

Raspberry balsamic cupcakes

Preparation time: 30 minutes (+ 20 minutes cooling time)
Cooking time: 25 minutes
Decorating time: 10 minutes
Makes: 12 standard cupcakes

225 g (8 oz/1½ cups) plain flour
1½ teaspoons baking powder
75 g (2¾ oz/⅓ cup, firmly packed) dark brown sugar
175 g (6 oz/½ cup) golden syrup
125 g (4½ oz) unsalted butter, softened
60 ml (2 fl oz/¼ cup) milk
3 eggs, at room temperature
1 teaspoon vanilla extract
250 ml (9 fl oz/1 cup) thick (double/heavy) cream

Raspberry balsamic syrup
200 g (7 oz/1⅔ cups) frozen raspberries
275 g (9¾ oz/1¼ cups) caster sugar
1½ tablespoons balsamic vinegar

1 Preheat oven to 170°C (325°F/Gas 3). Line 12 standard (80 ml/2½ fl oz/⅓ cup) muffin holes with paper cases.
2 Sift the flour and baking powder into a large bowl. Add the sugar, golden syrup, butter, milk, eggs and vanilla. Use electric beaters to beat on low speed until combined. Increase speed to medium and beat for 2–3 minutes or until well combined, very smooth and the mixture is paler in colour. Divide the mixture evenly among the paper cases then smooth the tops with the back of a teaspoon
3 Bake for 20–25 minutes, turning the tin around after 15 minutes, or until golden and a skewer inserted into the centre of a cupcake comes out clean. Allow to cool for 5 minutes in the tin before transferring to a wire rack to cool completely.
4 Meanwhile, to make the syrup, put the raspberries in a 23 cm (9½ in) non-stick frying pan over medium–high heat then sprinkle over the sugar. Stir gently after 1 minute to combine any sugar yet to dissolve. Drizzle over the vinegar and cook without stirring for 4–5 minutes or until syrupy (there should still be some whole raspberries). Remove the pan from the heat and set aside to cool.
5 To decorate, spoon a heaped teaspoonful of the cream onto the centre of each cupcake and use a teaspoon to spread it into a circle on top of the cake. Spoon over the syrup and serve immediately.

TIPS: Keep the syrup in an airtight container for up to 2 days.

Keep undecorated cupcakes in an airtight container in a cool place for up to 2 days. Decorate cupcakes with cream and syrup just before serving.

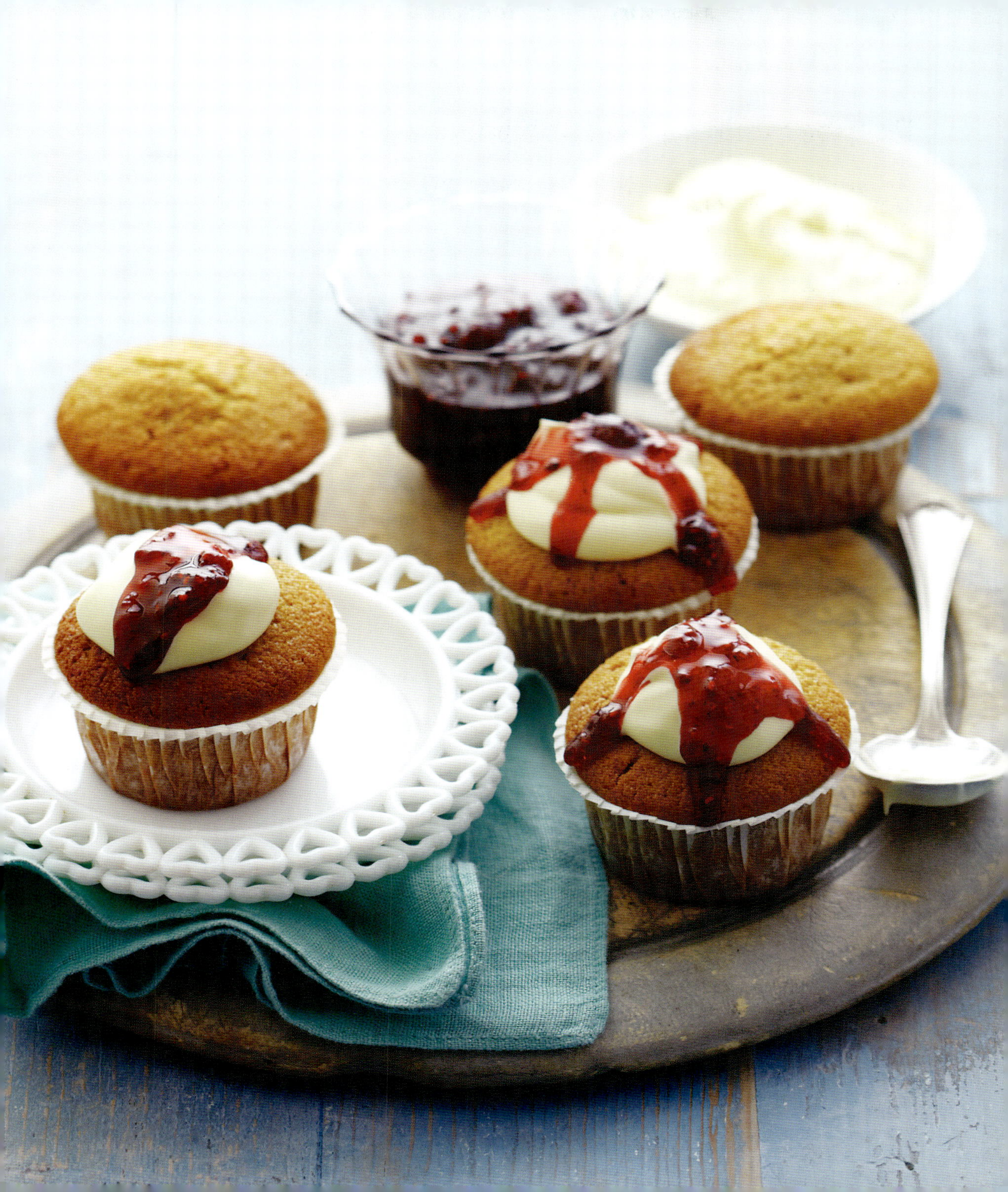

Plum & cardamom cakes

Preparation time: 20 minutes
Cooking time: 20 minutes
Decorating time: 5 minutes
Makes: 12 standard cupcakes

825 g (1 lb 13 oz) tinned plums in juice
125 g (4½ oz) unsalted butter, well softened
100 g (3½ oz/½ cup, lightly packed) soft brown sugar
55 g (2 oz/¼ cup) caster sugar
1 teaspoon vanilla extract
2 eggs, at room temperature
185 g (6½ oz/1¼ cups) plain flour
1 teaspoon baking powder
½ teaspoon ground cardamom
125 ml (4 fl oz/½ cup) milk
20 g (¾ oz) unsalted butter, melted
2 tablespoons coffee crystals
¼ teaspoon ground cardamom, extra

TIPS: Keep leftover plums in their syrup in an airtight container in the fridge for up to 4 days.

Keep cupcakes in an airtight container in the fridge for up to 2 days. Serve at room temperature.

1 Preheat oven to 190°C (375°F/Gas 5). Line 12 standard (80 ml/2½ fl oz/⅓ cup) muffin holes with paper cases.
2 Drain the plums, reserving the juice, and weigh out 200 g (7 oz) plums (see tip). Remove the stones and chop into 1.5 cm (⅝ in) pieces.
3 Use an electric mixer to beat the butter, sugars and vanilla together in a medium bowl on low speed for 2–3 minutes or until slightly paler in colour and creamy. Add the eggs, one at a time, beating well after each addition. Sift the flour, baking powder and cardamom over the top then add the milk. Use a wooden spoon to fold through until combined. Stir through two-thirds of the chopped plums. Divide the mixture evenly among the paper cases then smooth the tops with the back of a teaspoon. Top with the remaining chopped plums.
4 Bake for 20 minutes, turning the tin around after 10 minutes, or until golden and a skewer inserted into the centre of a cupcake comes out clean. Remove from the tin and transfer to a wire rack. Brush the warm cupcakes with the melted butter. Combine the coffee crystals and extra cardamom and sprinkle over the top.
5 Serve warm or at room temperature.

Caramel & walnut cupcakes

Preparation time: 25 minutes (+ cooling time)
Cooking time: 30 minutes
Decorating time: 10 minutes
Makes: 12 standard cupcakes

225 g (8 oz/1½ cups) plain flour
1½ teaspoons baking powder
75 g (2¾ oz/⅓ cup, firmly packed) dark brown sugar
175 g (6 oz/½ cup) golden syrup
125 g (4½ oz) unsalted butter, softened
60 ml (2 fl oz/¼ cup) milk
3 eggs, at room temperature
1 teaspoon vanilla extract
1 quantity caramel buttercream (see page 123)

Candied walnuts
115 g (4 oz/1 cup) walnut halves
1 teaspoon water
2 tablespoons pure icing sugar
1 teaspoon ground cinnamon

TIP: Keep iced and decorated cupcakes in an airtight container in the fridge for up to 2 days. Serve at room temperature.

1 Preheat oven to 170°C (325°F/Gas 3). Line 12 standard (80 ml/2½ fl oz/⅓ cup) muffin holes with paper cases.
2 Sift the flour and baking powder into a large bowl. Add the sugar, golden syrup, butter, milk, eggs and vanilla. Use electric beaters to beat on low speed until combined. Increase speed to medium and beat for 2–3 minutes or until well combined, very smooth and the mixture is paler in colour. Divide the mixture evenly among the paper cases then smooth the tops with the back of a teaspoon.
3 Bake for 20–25 minutes, turning the tin around after 15 minutes, or until golden and a skewer inserted into the centre of a cupcake comes out clean. Allow to cool for 5 minutes in the tin before transferring to a wire rack to cool completely.
4 Meanwhile, to make the candied walnuts, increase oven to 180°C (350°F/Gas 4). Line a small baking tray with baking paper. Put the walnuts in a small bowl and sprinkle with the water. Sift over the icing sugar and cinnamon and toss until well coated. Spread the nut mixture evenly over the baking tray. Bake for 5 minutes or until golden and caramelised. Set aside to cool completely.
5 To decorate, use a piping bag fitted with a 1 cm (½ in) plain nozzle to pipe the buttercream onto the cooled cupcakes. Decorate with the candied walnuts.

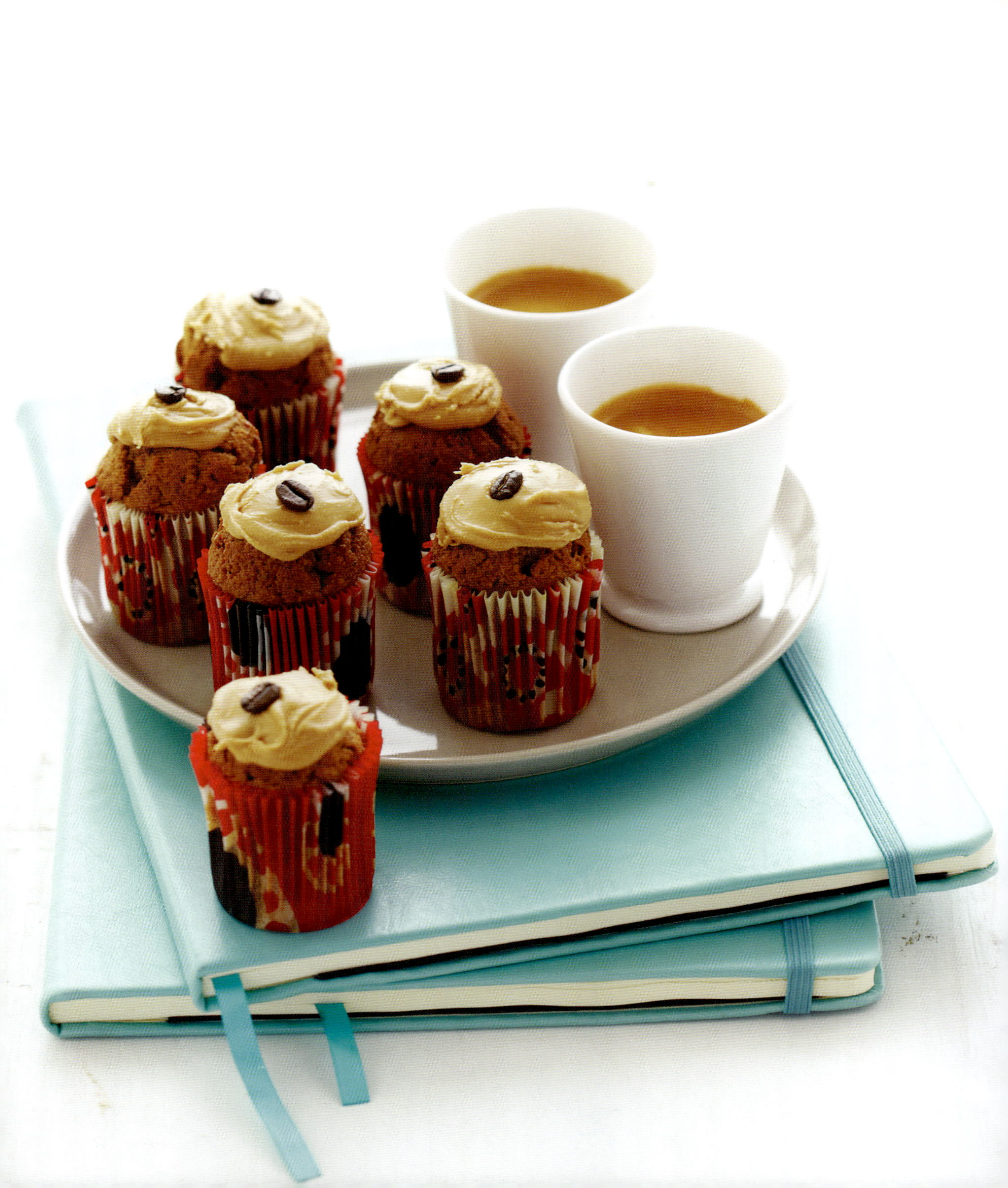

Espresso cakes

Preparation time: 25 minutes (+ cooling time)
Cooking time: 15 minutes
Decorating time: 15 minutes
Makes: 14 standard cupcakes

3 teaspoons instant coffee granules
2 tablespoons boiling water
110 g (3¾ oz/¾ cup) plain flour
1 teaspoon baking powder
165 g (5¾ oz/¾ cup) caster sugar
175 g (6 oz) unsalted butter, well softened
3 eggs, at room temperature
75 g (2¾ oz/⅔ cup) hazelnut meal
14 coffee beans

Coffee icing
210 g (7½ oz/1⅔ cups) pure icing sugar, sifted
1 teaspoon instant coffee granules
15 ml (½ fl oz/1 tablespoon) boiling water
½ teaspoon vanilla extract

1 Preheat oven to 170°C (325°F/Gas 3). Line 14 standard (80 ml/2½ fl oz/⅓ cup) muffin holes with paper cases.
2 Combine the coffee and boiling water in a small bowl. Set aside. Sift the flour and baking powder into a medium bowl. Add the sugar, butter and eggs. Use electric beaters to beat on low speed until just combined. Increase the speed to medium and beat for 1 minute or until well combined and smooth. Add the hazelnut meal and coffee mixture and use a large metal spoon to fold through until smooth. Divide the mixture evenly among the paper cases then smooth the tops with the back of a teaspoon.
3 Bake for 15 minutes, turning the tins around after 8 minutes, or until light golden and a skewer inserted into the centre of a cupcake comes out clean. Allow to cool for 5 minutes in the tins before transferring to a wire rack to cool completely.
4 To make the coffee icing, put the icing sugar in a medium heatproof bowl. Combine the coffee and boiling water in a small bowl. Add to the icing sugar and use a spatula or wooden spoon to stir until the mixture is smooth and has a heavy coating consistency. Add the vanilla and stir to combine. Set aside until cool and thick.
5 To decorate, place a heaped teaspoonful of the icing onto the top of a cupcake and spread with a palette knife. Place a whole coffee bean on top. Repeat with the remaining cupcakes, icing and coffee beans.

TIPS: Keep iced and decorated cupcakes in an airtight container in the fridge for up to 2 days. Serve at room temperature.

We used a tin with holes that had a 4 cm (1½ in) base, 5 cm (2 in) deep.

Rhubarb, hazelnut & brown sugar crumble cakes

Preparation time: 25 minutes
Cooking time: 40 minutes
Makes: 6 large cupcakes

melted butter, to grease
125 g (4½ oz) unsalted butter, softened
110 g (3¾ oz/½ cup, firmly packed) soft brown sugar
55 g (2 oz/¼ cup) caster sugar
1 teaspoon vanilla extract
2 eggs, at room temperature
150 g (5½ oz/1 cup) plain flour
1 teaspoon baking powder
25 g (1 oz/¼ cup) desiccated coconut
125 ml (4 fl oz/½ cup) milk
cream or vanilla ice cream, to serve

Rhubarb crumble topping
180 g (6¼ oz) thin stalks rhubarb, trimmed (see tip), cut into 1 cm (½ in) pieces
2 teaspoons caster sugar
75 g (2¾ oz/½ cup) plain flour
50 g (1¾ oz) unsalted butter, chilled, chopped
40 g (1½ oz/¼ cup) hazelnuts, finely chopped
2 tablespoons caster sugar, extra

> **TIPS:** You will need 140 g (5 oz) trimmed rhubarb.
>
> Keep cupcakes in an airtight container in the fridge for up to 2 days. Warm in the oven or serve at room temperature.

1 Preheat oven to 190°C (375°F/Gas 5). Lightly grease 6 large (185 ml/6 fl oz/¾ cup) muffin holes and place two strips of baking paper at right angles in each hole to help remove the cupcakes.

2 To make the topping, put the rhubarb and sugar in a medium bowl and toss to combine. Put the flour, butter, hazelnuts and extra sugar in a medium bowl and use your fingertips to combine. Set aside.

3 Use an electric mixer to beat the butter, sugars and vanilla together in a medium bowl on low speed for 2–3 minutes or until slightly paler in colour and creamy. Add the eggs, one at a time, beating well after each addition. Sift the flour and baking powder over the top, add the coconut and milk and fold through with a wooden spoon until just combined.

4 Divide the mixture evenly among the muffin holes then smooth the tops with the back of a teaspoon. Top with the rhubarb in an even layer. Sprinkle the crumble topping on top.

5 Bake for 40 minutes, turning the tin around after 20 minutes, or until golden and a skewer inserted into the centre of a cupcake comes out clean. Set aside to cool for 5 minutes in the tin. Loosen the edges, then carefully remove using the paper strips to pull the cakes out.

6 Serve warm with cream or ice cream.

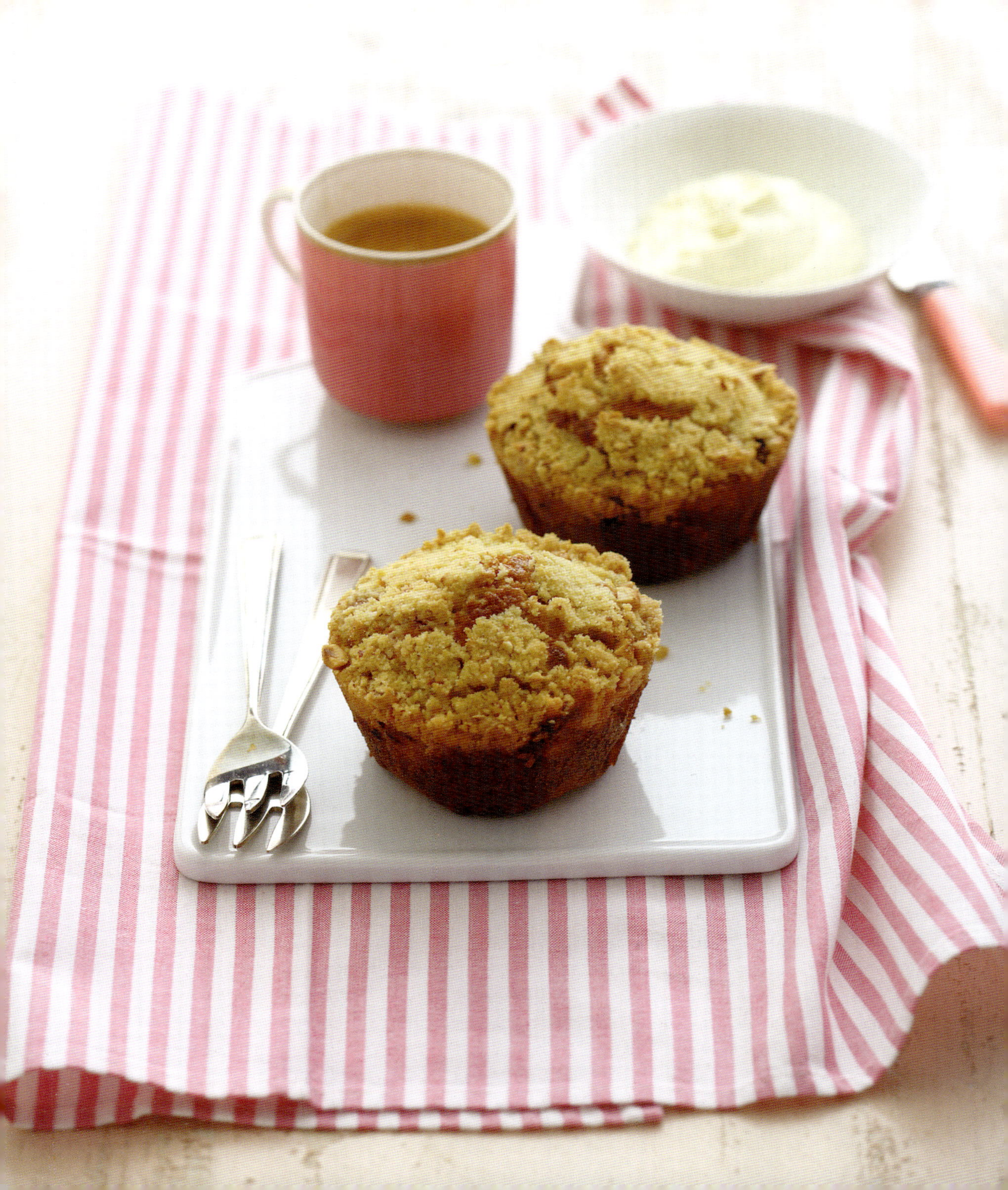

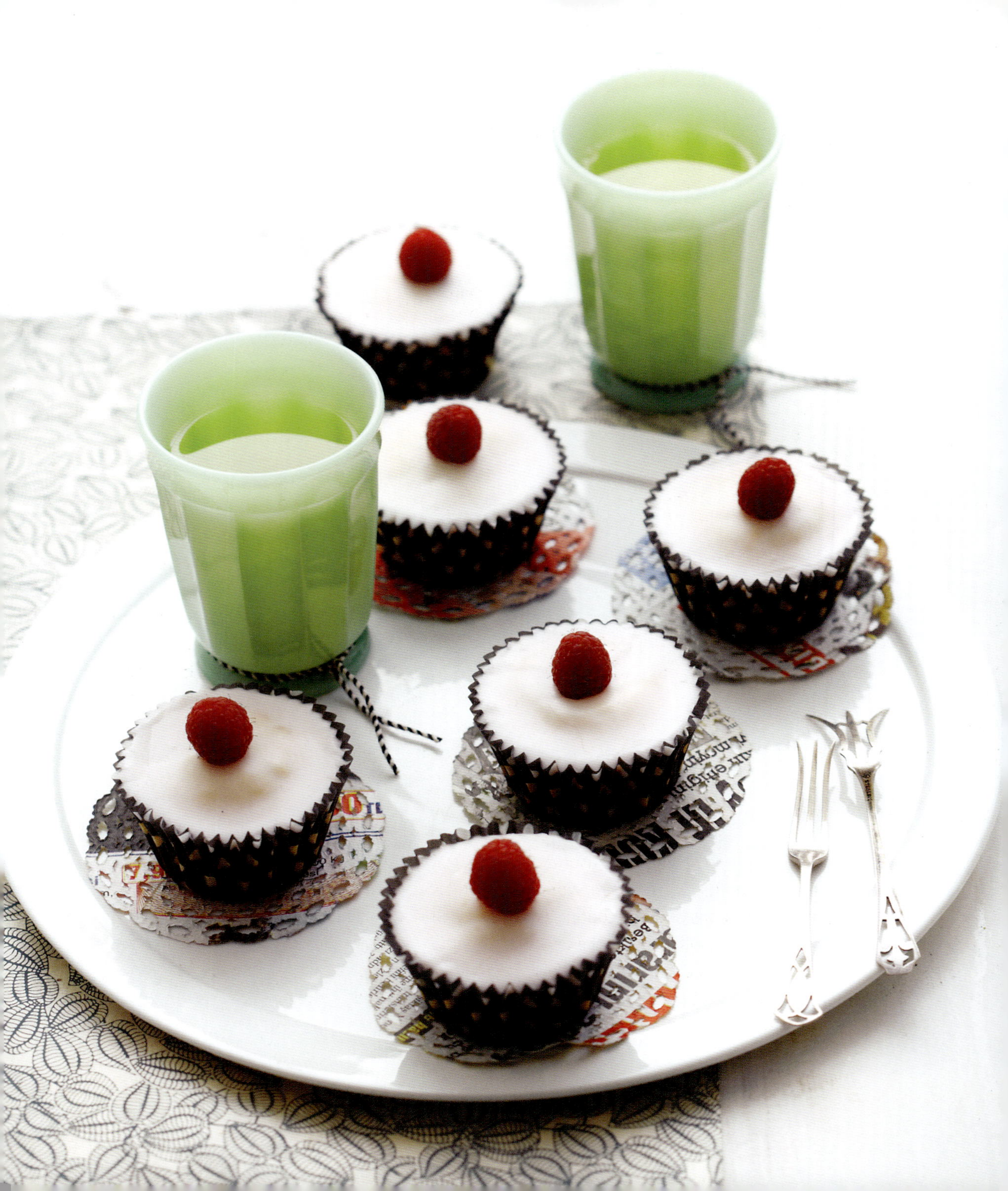

Peach & raspberry cupcakes

Preparation time: 20 minutes
Cooking time: 20 minutes
Decorating time: 20 minutes
Makes: 10 standard cupcakes

110 g (3¾ oz/¾ cup) plain flour
¾ teaspoon baking powder
110 g (3¾ oz/½ cup) caster sugar
125 g (4½ oz) unsalted butter, well softened
2 eggs, at room temperature
½ teaspoon vanilla extract
2 tablespoons milk
125 g (4½ oz/1 cup) fresh raspberries
70 g (2½ oz/½ cup) dried peaches, chopped into 1 cm (½ in) dice

Icing
300 g (10½ oz) pure icing sugar, sifted
1½ tablespoons hot water
3 teaspoons strained freshly squeezed lemon juice

TIP: These cupcakes are best served on the day of making.

1 Preheat oven to 160°C (315°F/Gas 2–3). Line 10 standard (80 ml/2½ fl oz/⅓ cup) muffin holes with paper cases.
2 Sift the flour and baking powder into a medium bowl. Add the sugar, butter, eggs, vanilla and milk. Use electric beaters to beat for 2 minutes on low speed until combined and smooth.
3 Set aside 11 of the raspberries for the icing and decoration, add the remaining raspberries and peaches to the bowl and use a spatula to gently fold through. Divide the mixture evenly among the paper cases then smooth the tops with the back of a teaspoon.
4 Bake for 15–20 minutes, turning the tin around after 8 minutes, or until light golden and a skewer inserted into the centre of a cupcake comes out clean. Allow to cool for 5 minutes in the tin before transferring to a wire rack to cool completely.
5 To make the icing, place 1 of the reserved raspberries in a small sieve over a bowl and use the back of a teaspoon to extract a little raspberry juice (to lightly colour the icing). Add the icing sugar to the bowl and use a spatula or wooden spoon to slowly stir in the hot water until the mixture is smooth and has a heavy coating consistency. Stir in the lemon juice.
6 To decorate, working with one cupcake at a time, place 2 teaspoons of the icing on top of a cupcake. Tap the base on a bench to gently spread the icing over the cake to form a circle of icing right to the edge of the cupcake paper. Top with a reserved raspberry. Repeat with the remaining cupcakes, icing and raspberries.

Orange white chocolate cupcakes

Preparation time: 20 minutes
Cooking time: 30 minutes
Decorating time: 5 minutes
Makes: 6 large cupcakes

melted butter, for greasing
125 g (4½ oz) unsalted butter, chopped, softened
110 g (3¾ oz/½ cup) caster sugar
1 teaspoon finely grated orange zest
2 eggs, at room temperature
65 g (2½ oz/¼ cup) sour cream
150 g (5½ oz/1 cup) plain flour, plus extra, to dust
1 teaspoon baking powder
100 g (3½ oz) white chocolate, melted
thick (double/heavy) cream, to serve
1 quantity candied orange zest (see page 119), cut into wide strips

Orange liqueur syrup
220 g (7¾ oz/1 cup) caster sugar
185 ml (6 fl oz/¾ cup) strained freshly squeezed orange juice
60 ml (2 fl oz/¼ cup) orange liqueur (Grand Marnier)

> **TIP:** Keep cupcakes in an airtight container in the fridge for up to 2 days. Serve at room temperature.

1 Preheat oven to 180°C (350°F/Gas 4). Grease and flour 6 large (185 ml/6 fl oz/¾ cup) muffin holes and line the bases with rounds of baking paper.
2 Use an electric mixer to beat the butter, sugar and orange zest together in a medium bowl until pale and creamy. Add the eggs, one at a time, beating well after each addition. Beat in the sour cream. Sift the flour and baking powder into a medium bowl. With the mixer on low speed, add the flour and mix until combined. Add the melted chocolate and stir to combine. Divide the mixture evenly among the muffin holes then smooth the tops with the back of a teaspoon.
3 Bake for 20–25 minutes, turning the tin around after 15 minutes, or until golden and a skewer inserted into the centre of a cupcake comes out clean.
4 Meanwhile, to make the syrup, combine the sugar and orange juice in a small saucepan, stirring over low heat until the sugar dissolves. Bring to the boil then remove from the heat and cool slightly. Stir in the liqueur. Drizzle half the syrup over the warm cupcakes and allow to soak up the syrup. When cool remove from the tin. Place on a serving platter and drizzle with a little more syrup.
5 Serve the cupcakes warm, topped with a dollop of cream and a little candied orange zest.

Cinnamon & fig cupcakes

Preparation time: 30 minutes
Cooking time: 12 minutes
Makes: 48 mini cupcakes

225 g (8 oz/1½ cups) plain flour
1½ teaspoons baking powder
1 teaspoon ground cinnamon
165 g (5¾ oz/¾ cup) caster sugar, plus 1 teaspoon extra
125 g (4½ oz) unsalted butter, chopped, softened
60 ml (2 fl oz/¼ cup) milk
3 eggs, at room temperature
1 teaspoon vanilla extract
4 fresh figs (50 g/1¾ oz each) or 75 g (2¾ oz/⅓ cup) dried figs, cut into small wedges

1 Preheat oven to 170°C (325°F/Gas 3). Line 48 mini (20 ml/½ fl oz/1 tablespoon) muffin holes with paper cases.
2 Sift the flour and baking powder into a large bowl. Add the cinnamon, sugar, butter, milk, eggs and vanilla. Use electric beaters to beat on low speed until combined. Increase speed to medium–high and beat for 2–3 minutes or until well combined, very smooth and the mixture is paler in colour.
3 Divide the mixture evenly among the paper cases, top with the figs and sprinkle with the extra sugar.
4 Bake for 12 minutes, turning the tins around after 7 minutes, or until a skewer inserted into the centre of a cupcake comes out clean. Allow to cool for 5 minutes in the tins before transferring to a wire rack to cool completely.

TIP: Keep cupcakes in an airtight container in the fridge for up to 2 days. Serve at room temperature.

Mini Christmas pudding cakes

Preparation time: 20 minutes (+ overnight soaking time + cooling time)
Cooking time: 40 minutes
Decorating time: 20 minutes
Makes: 24 standard cupcakes

510 g (1 lb 2 oz/3 cups) sultanas (golden raisins)
385 g (13½ oz/2¼ cups) raisins
245 g (9 oz/1⅔ cups) currants
240 g (8¾ oz/1 cup) quartered glacé cherries
250 ml (9 fl oz/1 cup) brandy or rum
250 g (9 oz) unsalted butter, softened, plus extra, melted, for greasing
220 g (7¾ oz/1 cup, firmly packed) dark brown sugar
2 tablespoons apricot jam
2 tablespoons light treacle or golden syrup
1 tablespoon finely grated lemon or orange zest
4 eggs, at room temperature
410 g (14½ oz/2¾ cups) plain (all-purpose) flour
1 teaspoon each of ground ginger, mixed spice and ground cinnamon
silver cachous, to decorate

Royal icing
2 egg whites, at room temperature
500 g (1 lb 2 oz/4 cups) pure icing sugar, sifted
1–2 tablespoons strained freshly squeezed lemon juice

TIP: Keep un-iced cupcakes in an airtight container in a cool place for up to 1 week. Keep iced and decorated cupcakes in an airtight container in a cool place for up to 2 days.

1 Put the fruit and brandy in a medium bowl, stir to combine and leave to soak overnight.
2 Preheat oven to 150°C (300°F/Gas 2). Grease 24 standard (80 ml/2½ fl oz/⅓ cup) muffin holes.
3 Use an electric mixer to beat the butter and sugar until just combined. Add the jam, treacle and zest and mix to combine. Add the eggs, one at a time, beating well after each addition. Sift the flour and spices together. Stir the soaked fruit and the flour alternately into the butter mixture in two separate batches each. Stir until combined. Divide the mixture evenly among the muffin holes, then smooth the tops with the back of a teaspoon.
4 Bake for 40 minutes or until a skewer inserted into the centre of a cupcake comes out clean. Allow to cool completely in the tins then turn out the cakes so that the base becomes the top.
5 To make the royal icing, lightly beat the egg whites with a wooden spoon. Gradually add the icing sugar, whisking to a smooth paste. Slowly add enough of the lemon juice until the icing is slightly runny.
6 To decorate, use a palette knife to spread each cake with the icing, letting some drizzle down the sides. Decorate with cachous.

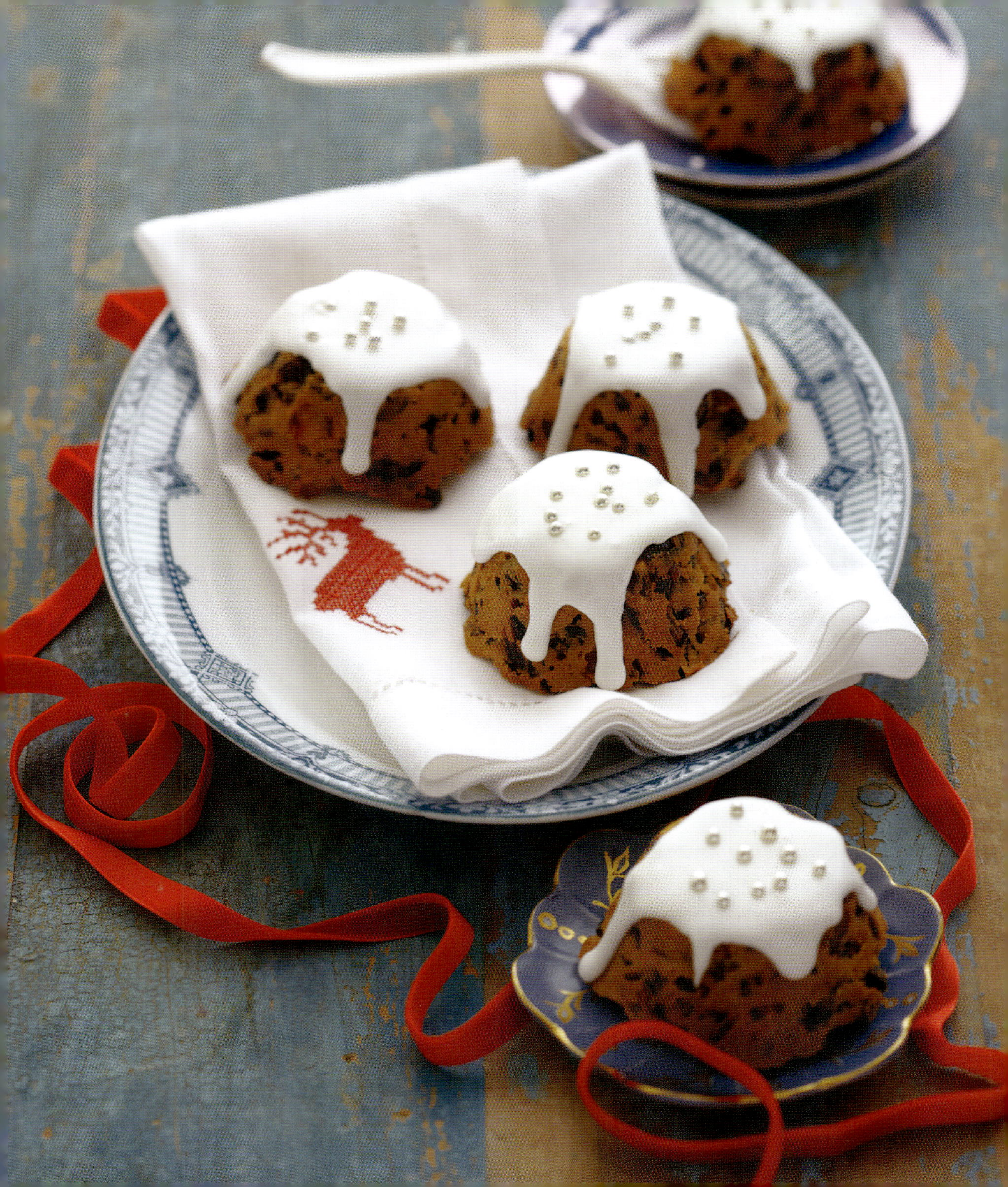

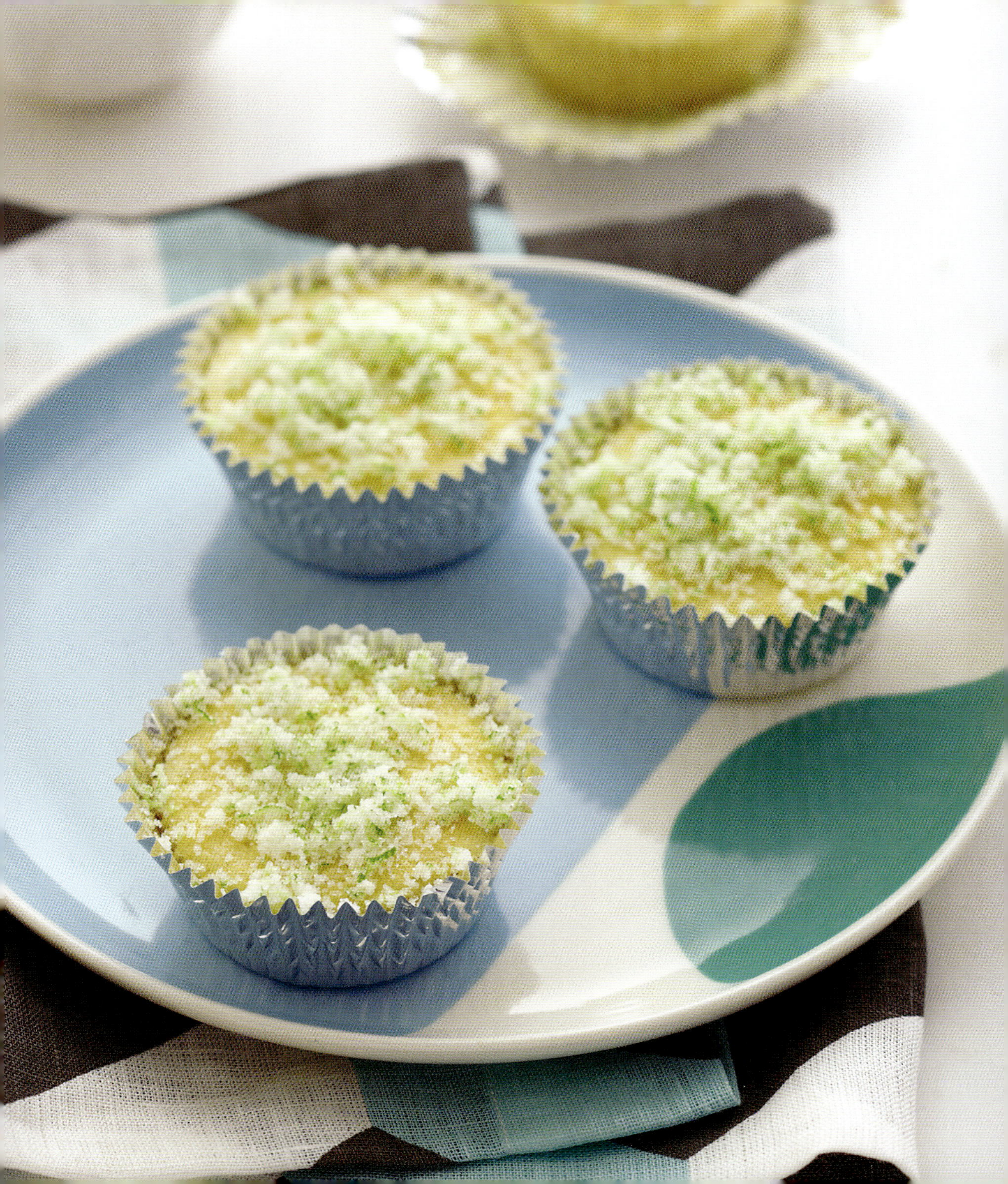

Lime delicious cupcakes

Preparation time: 20 minutes
Cooking time: 20 minutes
Makes: 10 standard cupcakes

40 g (1½ oz) unsalted butter, softened
165 g (5¾ oz/¾ cup) caster sugar
2 eggs, at room temperature, separated
finely grated zest of 2 limes
110 g (3¾ oz/¾ cup) plain flour
½ teaspoon baking powder
60 ml (2 fl oz/¼ cup) strained freshly squeezed lime juice
170 ml (5½ fl oz/⅔ cup) milk

Lime sugar
2 tablespoons granulated white sugar
finely grated zest of 1 lime

> **TIPS:** Serve cupcakes with thick (double/heavy) cream or vanilla ice cream.
>
> Keep cupcakes in an airtight container in the fridge for up to 2 days. Serve at room temperature.

1 Preheat oven to 180°C (350°F/Gas 4). Line 10 standard (80 ml/2½ fl oz/⅓ cup) muffin holes with foil cases.
2 To make the lime sugar, combine the sugar and lime zest in a small bowl.
3 Use an electric mixer to beat the butter and sugar in a medium bowl for 3 minutes or until well combined. Add the egg yolks and lime zest and beat for 1 minute or until well combined. Sift the flour and baking powder over the top then add the lime juice. Beat until combined while slowly adding the milk. Continue beating until smooth.
4 Put the egg whites in a medium clean, dry bowl and whisk until stiff peaks form. Use a large metal spoon to fold one-third of the egg white gently into the lime mixture, then add the remainder and combine gently. Divide the mixture evenly among the foil cases then smooth the tops with the back of a teaspoon.
5 Bake for 18–20 minutes, turning the tin around after 8 minutes, or until light golden and just set. Allow to cool for 5 minutes in the tin before transferring to a wire rack and sprinkling with the lime sugar. Serve warm or at room temperature.

Rich dark chocolate cupcakes

Preparation time: 25 minutes
Cooking time: 25 minutes
Decorating time: 20 minutes
Makes: 18 standard cupcakes

150 g (5½ oz) unsalted butter, chopped
200 g (7 oz/1¼ cups) dark chocolate melts
225 g (8 oz/1½ cups) self-raising flour
30 g (1 oz/¼ cup) unsweetened cocoa powder
275 g (9¾ oz/1¼ cups) caster sugar
2 eggs, at room temperature, lightly beaten
185 ml (6 fl oz/¾ cup) water
chocolate curls (see tip) or grated chocolate, to decorate

Chocolate topping
250 g (9 oz) dark chocolate, chopped
40 g (1½ oz) unsalted butter

TIPS: To make chocolate curls, use a sharp knife to shave curls from a block of chocolate.

Keep iced and decorated cupcakes in an airtight container in the fridge for up to 2 days. Serve at room temperature.

1 Preheat oven to 160°C (315°F/Gas 2–3). Line 18 standard (80 ml/2½ fl oz/⅓ cup) muffin holes with paper cases.
2 Put the butter and chocolate melts in a small heatproof bowl. Sit the bowl over a saucepan of simmering water, making sure the base of the bowl doesn't touch the water. Stir constantly until the chocolate melts. Remove from the heat and allow to cool slightly.
3 Sift the flour and cocoa powder into a large bowl. In a separate large bowl, combine the cooled chocolate mixture, sugar and egg, then add the water and mix well with a large spoon. Add to the dry ingredients and stir until well combined. Divide the mixture evenly among the paper cases.
4 Bake for 20–25 minutes or until a skewer inserted into the centre of a cupcake comes out clean. Allow to cool for 5 minutes in the tins before transferring to a wire rack to cool completely.
5 To make the chocolate topping, put the chocolate and butter in a small heatproof bowl. Sit the bowl over a saucepan of simmering water, making sure the base of the bowl doesn't touch the water. Stir constantly until the chocolate melts. Remove from the heat and allow to cool.
6 To decorate, spread the topping over the cupcakes and top with the chocolate curls.

Sticky date cupcakes

Preparation time: 25 minutes
Cooking time: 30 minutes
Makes: 6 large cupcakes

melted butter, to grease
245 g (9 oz/1½ cups) pitted dates, chopped
250 ml (9 fl oz/1 cup) water
1 teaspoon bicarbonate of soda
60 g (2¼ oz) unsalted butter, chopped
225 g (8 oz/1½ cups) self-raising flour
125 g (4½ oz/⅔ cup, lightly packed) soft brown sugar
2 eggs, at room temperature, lightly beaten
vanilla ice cream, to serve

Sauce
2 tablespoons golden syrup or maple syrup
185 ml (6 fl oz/¾ cup) pouring (whipping) cream
90 g (3¼ oz) unsalted butter, chopped
150 g (5½ oz/¾ cup, lightly packed) soft brown sugar

1 Preheat oven to 180°C (350°F/Gas 4). Grease 6 large (185 ml/6 fl oz/¾ cup) muffin holes.
2 Put the dates and water in a saucepan and bring to the boil. Remove from the heat and stir in the bicarbonate of soda. Add the butter and stir until melted.
3 Sift the flour into a large bowl, then add the sugar and stir to combine. Make a well in the centre, add the date mixture and egg and stir with a wooden spoon until just combined. Divide the mixture evenly among the muffin holes.
4 Bake for 20 minutes or until a skewer inserted into the centre of a cupcake comes out clean. Allow to cool in the tin for 10 minutes then transfer to serving plates.
5 Meanwhile, to make the sauce, put the golden syrup, cream, butter and sugar in a small saucepan and stir over low heat for 3–4 minutes or until the sugar dissolves. Bring to the boil, then reduce the heat and simmer, stirring occasionally, for 2 minutes.
6 Pierce the tops of the warm cupcakes a few times with a skewer, then drizzle with the sauce. Serve with ice cream.

TIPS: Serve cupcakes warm or at room temperature. If not serving them straight away, do not pour over the sauce but reheat when ready to serve.

Keep cupcakes (without the sauce) in an airtight container in the fridge for up to 2 days.

Intense mandarin cupcakes

Preparation time: 30 minutes (+ 20 minutes cooling time)
Cooking time: 30 minutes
Decorating time: 5 minutes
Makes: 12 standard cupcakes

125 g (4½ oz) unsalted butter, well softened
150 g (5½ oz/⅔ cup) caster sugar
finely grated zest of 2 mandarins
3 eggs, at room temperature, separated
225 g (8 oz/1½ cups) plain flour
1½ teaspoons baking powder
2 tablespoons strained freshly squeezed mandarin juice
80 ml (2½ fl oz/⅓ cup) milk

Intense mandarin jam
2 small, thin-skinned mandarins (200 g/7 oz in total), unpeeled
165 g (5¾ oz/¾ cup) caster sugar
½ lemon, juice freshly squeezed

> **TIPS:** If the jam becomes too firm, place the bowl over a saucepan of hot water.
>
> Keep cupcakes (without the jam) in an airtight container in the fridge for up to 2 days. Serve at room temperature.

1 Preheat oven to 180°C (350°F/Gas 4). Line 12 standard (80 ml/2½ fl oz/⅓ cup) muffin holes with paper cases.

2 Use an electric mixer to beat the butter, sugar and mandarin zest together in a medium bowl on low speed for 1–2 minutes or until light and creamy. Add the egg yolks and beat until combined. Sift over the flour and baking powder, add the mandarin juice, milk and egg whites and beat for 1 minute or until combined and smooth. Divide the mixture evenly among the paper cases then smooth the tops with the back of a teaspoon.

3 Bake for 20 minutes, turning the tin around after 10 minutes, or until light golden and a skewer inserted into the centre of a cupcake comes out clean. Allow to cool for 5 minutes in the tin before transferring to a wire rack.

4 Meanwhile, to make the mandarin jam, slice the whole mandarins into thin wedges about 1 cm (½ in) thick, discarding any pith from the core. Put the mandarin wedges in a small saucepan over low heat with the sugar and lemon juice and stir gently to dissolve the sugar. Increase the heat to medium and simmer rapidly for 5–10 minutes or until syrupy and the mandarin skin is translucent. Transfer to a heatproof bowl and set aside to cool for 20 minutes.

5 To decorate, brush the warm cakes with the syrup and top with the mandarin pieces. Serve warm or at room temperature.

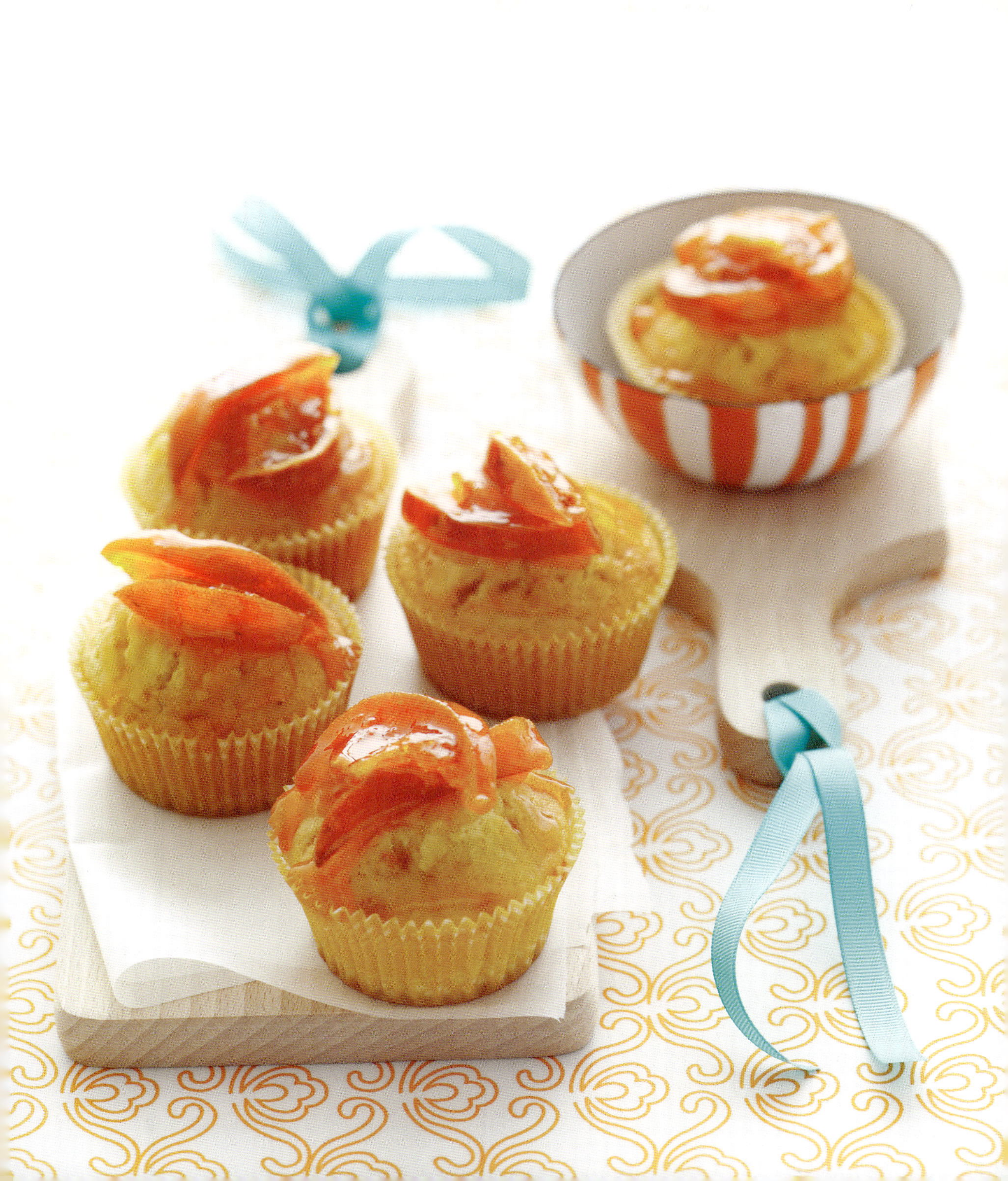

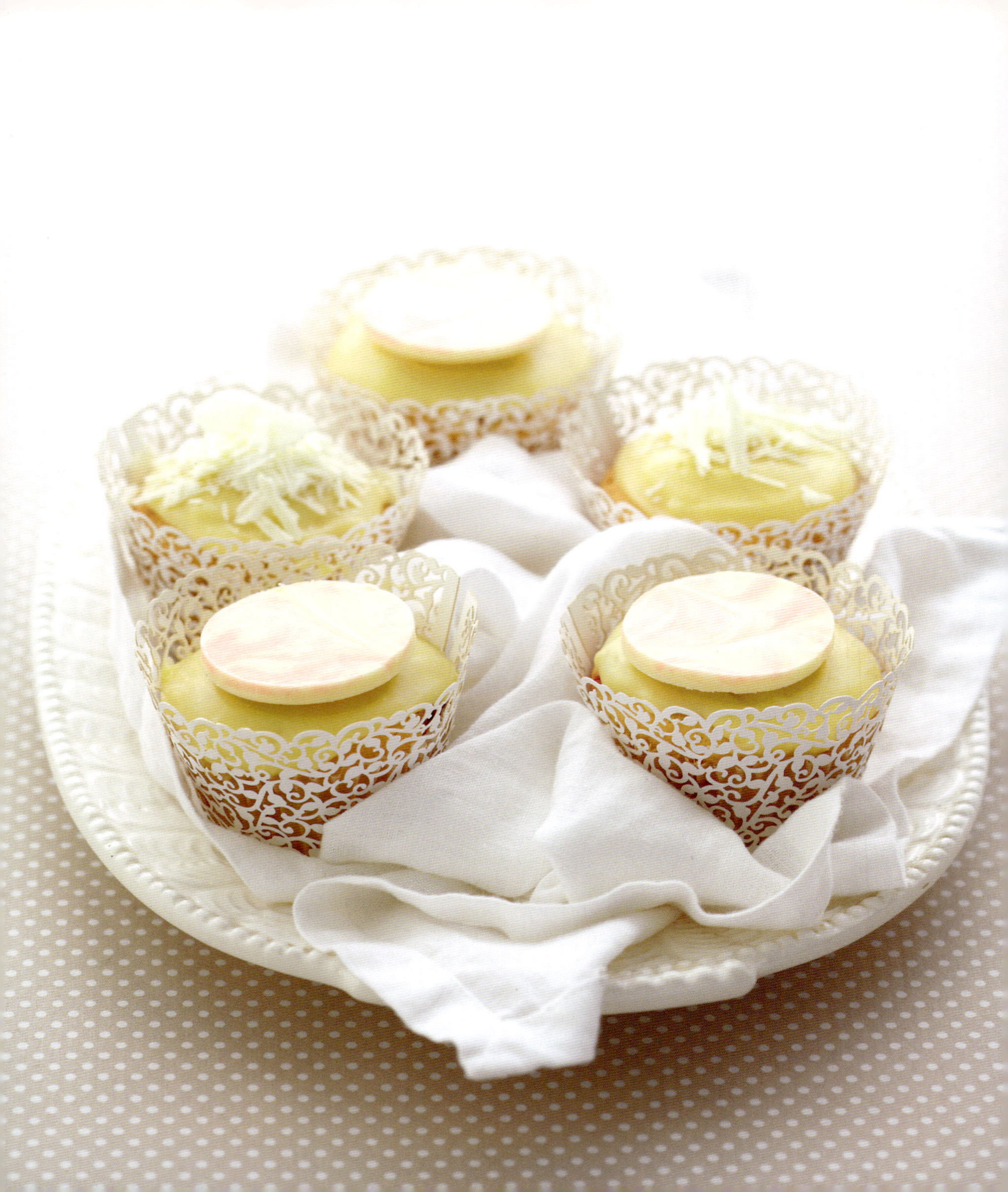

Coconut & raspberry cupcakes

Preparation time: 35 minutes (+ 40 minutes setting time)
Cooking time: 25 minutes
Decorating time: 15 minutes
Makes: 12 standard cupcakes

225 g (8 oz/1½ cups) plain flour
1½ teaspoons baking powder
165 g (5¾ oz/¾ cup) caster sugar
125 g (4½ oz) unsalted butter, softened
60 ml (2 fl oz/¼ cup) coconut milk
3 eggs, at room temperature
1 teaspoon coconut essence
155 g (5½ oz/1¼ cups) unthawed frozen or fresh raspberries
300 g (10½ oz) white chocolate, melted
pink food colouring
1 quantity white chocolate ganache (see page 120), at room temperature

TIP: Keep iced and decorated cupcakes in an airtight container in the fridge for up to 2 days. Serve at room temperature.

1 Preheat oven to 160°C (315°F/Gas 2–3). Line 12 standard (80 ml/2½ fl oz/⅓ cup) muffin holes with paper cases.

2 Sift the flour and baking powder into a large bowl. Add the sugar, butter, coconut milk, eggs and coconut essence. Use electric beaters to beat on low speed until combined. Increase speed to medium and beat for 2–3 minutes or until well combined, very smooth and the mixture is paler in colour. Add 1 cup of the raspberries and use a metal spoon to fold in gently. Divide the mixture evenly among the paper cases then smooth the tops with the back of a teaspoon.

3 Bake for 25 minutes, turning the tin around after 15 minutes, or until golden and a skewer inserted into the centre of a cupcake comes out clean. Allow to cool for 5 minutes in the tin before transferring to a wire rack to cool completely.

4 Divide the melted chocolate into two portions and tint one with the pink food colouring to desired colour. Allow to cool until it is just spreadable, around 15 minutes. Put a 30 cm (12 in) long piece of baking paper on a baking tray and pour the uncoloured chocolate onto the paper. Use a palette knife to spread gently to 3–4 mm (⅛ in) thick. Put spoonfuls of the pink chocolate on top and use a skewer to gently swirl. Set aside for 30 minutes or until firm but not hard. Use a 4.5 cm (1¾ in) round cutter to cut out 12 rounds from the chocolate but do not lift them from the paper. Place the tray in the fridge for 10 minutes or until the chocolate is hard then remove the rounds and set aside on a tray.

5 To decorate, place 2 teaspoons of the ganache on top of a cooled cupcake. Spread gently with a palette knife to cover the top of the cupcake. Repeat with the remaining cupcakes and ganache. Top with the chocolate rounds.

Basics

Vanilla cupcakes

Preparation time: 15 minutes
Cooking time: 25 minutes
Makes: 12 standard cupcakes

melted butter (optional), to grease
225 g (8 oz/1½ cups) plain flour
1½ teaspoons baking powder
165 g (5¾ oz/¾ cup) caster sugar
125 g (4½ oz) unsalted butter, chopped, softened
60 ml (2 fl oz/¼ cup) milk
3 eggs, at room temperature
1 teaspoon vanilla extract

TIP: These cupcakes can be stored in an airtight container in a cool place for up to 2 days.

1 Preheat oven to 160°C (315°F/Gas 2–3). Grease or line 12 standard (80 ml/2½ fl oz/⅓ cup) muffin holes with paper cases.
2 Sift the flour and baking powder into a large bowl. Add the sugar, butter, milk, eggs and vanilla. Use electric beaters to beat on low speed until combined. Increase speed to medium–high and beat for 2–3 minutes or until well combined, very smooth and the mixture is paler in colour. Divide the mixture evenly among the muffin holes then smooth the tops with the back of a teaspoon.
3 Bake for 20–25 minutes, turning the tin around after 15 minutes, or until golden and a skewer inserted into the centre of a cupcake comes out clean. Allow to cool for 5 minutes in the tin before transferring to a wire rack to cool completely.

Size variations

Mini cupcakes – Makes: 48
Divide the mixture among 48 mini (20 ml/½ fl oz/1 tablespoon) muffin tins greased or lined with 2 cm (¾ in) deep x 3 cm (1¼ in) base paper cases. Bake at 160°C (315°F/Gas 2–3) for 15 minutes.

Patty pan cupcakes – Makes: 24
Divide the mixture among 24 flat-based (40 ml/1¼ fl oz) patty pan holes greased or lined with 2.5 cm (1 in) deep x 4.5 cm (1¾ in) base paper cases. Bake at 160°C (315°F/Gas 2–3) for 20 minutes.

Large cupcakes – Makes: 6
Divide the mixture among 6 large (Texan) (185 ml/6 fl oz/¾ cup) muffin holes greased or lined with 4 cm (1½ in) deep x 6 cm (2½ in) base paper cases. Bake at 160°C (315°F/Gas 2–3) for 25–30 minutes.

Flavour variations

Chocolate cupcakes – replace 35 g (1¼ oz/¼ cup) of the flour with 30 g (1 oz/¼ cup) unsweetened cocoa powder and sift with the flour and baking powder.
Orange cupcakes – replace the vanilla extract with finely grated zest of 1 orange.
Lemon cupcakes – replace the vanilla extract with finely grated zest of 2 lemons.

Gluten-free cupcakes

Preparation time: 15 minutes
Cooking time: 25 minutes
Makes: 12 standard cupcakes

> 200 g (7 oz/1½ cups) gluten-free self-raising flour
> 165 g (5¾ oz/¾ cup) caster sugar
> 150 g (5 ½ oz) unsalted butter, softened
> 60 ml (2 fl oz/¼ cup) milk
> 3 eggs, at room temperature
> 1 teaspoon vanilla extract

1 Preheat oven to 160°C (315°F/Gas 2–3). Grease or line 12 standard (80 ml/2½ fl oz/⅓ cup) muffin holes with paper cases.
2 Sift the flour and 55 g (20 oz/¼ cup) of the sugar into a bowl. Use electric beaters to beat the butter in a small bowl for 4–5 minutes or until pale and creamy. Gradually beat in the flour mixture and milk until just combined. Transfer to a large bowl.
3 Use electric beaters with a whisk attachment to whisk the eggs, vanilla and remaining sugar in a medium bowl for about 5–6 minutes or until very thick and pale and tripled in volume. Use a spatula or large metal spoon to stir half the egg mixture into the flour mixture until combined. Fold in the remaining egg mixture until just combined. Divide the mixture evenly among the muffin holes then smooth the tops with the back of a teaspoon.
4 Bake for 25–30 munutes or until golden and a skewer inserted into the centre of a cupcake comes out clean. Allow to cool for 5 minutes in the tin before transferring to a wire rack to cool completely.

> **TIPS:** These cupcakes can be stored in an airtight container in a cool place for up to 2 days.
>
> For flavour and size variations, you can follow the suggestions listed on pages 116–117.

Royal icing

Preparation time: 10 minutes
Makes: 160 ml (5¼ fl oz/⅔ cup)

> 1 egg white
> 1 teaspoon strained freshly squeezed lemon juice
> 185 g (6½ oz/1½ cups) pure icing sugar, sifted

1 Combine the egg white and lemon juice in a medium bowl. Use an electric mixer with a whisk attachment to whisk until foamy.
2 With the motor running, add the icing sugar, 60 g (2¼ oz/½ cup) at a time, whisking well after each addition. Continue whisking until the mixture forms a smooth and glossy icing that holds its shape.

> **TIP:** To prevent a crust forming on the top of the icing, cover the surface with plastic wrap. Keep in a cool place for up to 1 day.

Candied citrus zest

Preparation time: 10 minutes (+ 30 minutes standing time)
Cooking time: 15 minutes
Makes: 2 tablespoons

> 2 tablespoons orange, lemon or lime zest strips (see tip)
> 110 g (3¾ oz/½ cup) sugar
> 80 ml (2½ fl oz/⅓ cup) water

1 Put the zest and enough water to cover in a small saucepan. Bring to the boil over medium heat. Drain and repeat. Drain well.
2 Combine the sugar and water in the same pan. Stir over low heat until the sugar dissolves. Add the zest and bring to a simmer. Simmer for 10 minutes, occasionally stirring with a fork to separate the strands, or until translucent and tender. Drain and spread the zest on a wire rack. Set aside for 30 minutes or until dry.

> **TIP:** To make the citrus zest strips, remove the zest from the fruit using a vegetable peeler. Remove any white pith from the zest with a small, sharp knife and then cut the zest into thin strips.

Cream cheese frosting

Preparation time: 15 minutes
Makes: 1¼ cups

> 250 g (9 oz) cream cheese, at room temperature, chopped
> 40 g (1½ oz/⅓ cup) pure icing sugar, sifted
> 1½ tablespoons strained freshly squeezed lemon juice

Use electric beaters to beat the cream cheese in a medium bowl for 30 seconds or until smooth. Add the icing sugar and lemon juice and beat for another 1–2 minutes or until smooth, well combined and a good spreading consistency.

Dark chocolate ganache

Preparation time: 5 minutes (+ 30–60 minutes chilling time)
Makes: 1¼ cups

> 250 g (9 oz) good-quality dark chocolate, chopped
> 185 ml (6 fl oz/¾ cup) pouring (whipping) cream

1 Put the chocolate in a medium heatproof bowl and set aside. Heat the cream in a small saucepan over medium heat until simmering. Pour the cream over the chocolate and set aside for 2–3 minutes. Stir until the chocolate melts and the mixture is well combined.
2 Refrigerate for 30–60 minutes, stirring often, or until thickened to a thick, spreadable consistency.

> **TIP:** Keep ganache in the fridge for up to 2 days. Bring to room temperature when ready to use.

Flavour variations

Milk chocolate ganache – replace the dark chocolate with milk chocolate.
White chocolate ganache – replace the dark chocolate with white chocolate.

Glacé icing

Preparation time: 5 minutes
Makes: 1 cup

>	405 g (14¼ oz/3¼ cups) pure icing sugar, sifted
>	60 ml (2 fl oz/¼ cup) room temperature water, approximately
>	1 teaspoon vanilla extract

Put the icing sugar in a medium heatproof bowl. Use a spatula or wooden spoon to slowly stir in the water until the mixture is smooth and has a heavy coating consistency. Stir in the vanilla. Add a little more water, if desired, to reach a lighter consistency. Use immediately.

Variations

Orange glacé icing – replace the water with room temperature strained freshly squeezed orange juice.
Lemon glacé icing – replace the water with room temperature strained freshly squeezed lemon juice.
Lime glacé icing – replace the water with room temperature strained freshly squeezed lime juice.

Chocolate glacé icing

Preparation time: 5 minutes
Makes: 1 cup

>	375 g (13 oz/3 cups) pure icing sugar
>	30 g (1 oz/¼ cup) unsweetened cocoa powder
>	60 ml (2 fl oz/¼ cup) room temperature water, approximately
>	1 teaspoon vanilla extract

Sift the icing sugar and cocoa powder together into a large bowl. Use a spatula or wooden spoon to slowly stir in the water until the mixture is smooth and has a heavy coating consistency. Stir in the vanilla. Add a little more water, if desired, to reach a lighter consistency.

Clockwise from bottom left: orange buttercream, lemon buttercream, chocolate buttercream, lime buttercream, caramel buttercream, vanilla buttercream.

Vanilla buttercream

Preparation time: 5 minutes
Makes: 2⅔ cups (enough for piping onto 12 standard cupcakes)

250 g (9 oz) unsalted butter, softened
2 tablespoons milk
3 teaspoons vanilla extract
405 g (14¼ oz/3⅓ cups) pure icing sugar, sifted
food colouring as desired (optional)

Use electric beaters to beat the butter in a medium bowl for 1–2 minutes or until pale and creamy. Add the milk, vanilla and half the icing sugar and beat until well combined. Add the remaining icing sugar and beat for 1–2 minutes or until smooth and creamy. Add food colouring to tint to desired colour, if using, and beat until just combined. Use as desired.

Flavour variations

Chocolate buttercream – reduce the icing sugar to 340 g (12 oz/2¾ cups). Sift 55 g (2 oz/½ cup) unsweetened cocoa powder with the remaining half of the icing sugar before adding with the second beating.
Orange buttercream – replace the vanilla extract with the finely grated zest of 1 orange.
Lemon buttercream – replace the vanilla extract with the finely grated zest of 2 lemons.
Lime buttercream – replace the vanilla extract with the finely grated zest of 3 limes.
Caramel buttercream – reduce the icing sugar to 250 g (9 oz/2 cups). Omit the milk. Add 110 g (3¾ oz/½ cup, firmly packed) soft brown sugar and 115 g (4 oz/⅓ cup) golden syrup with the vanilla for the first stage of beating. Then add the icing sugar in the second stage of beating.

> **TIP:** This buttercream is best used immediately. The consistency should be smooth and thick enough to hold its shape when piped. You can test by running your finger over the buttercream – it should hold its shape well but not be stiff. To adjust the consistency if necessary, beat in a little more milk or icing sugar as needed.

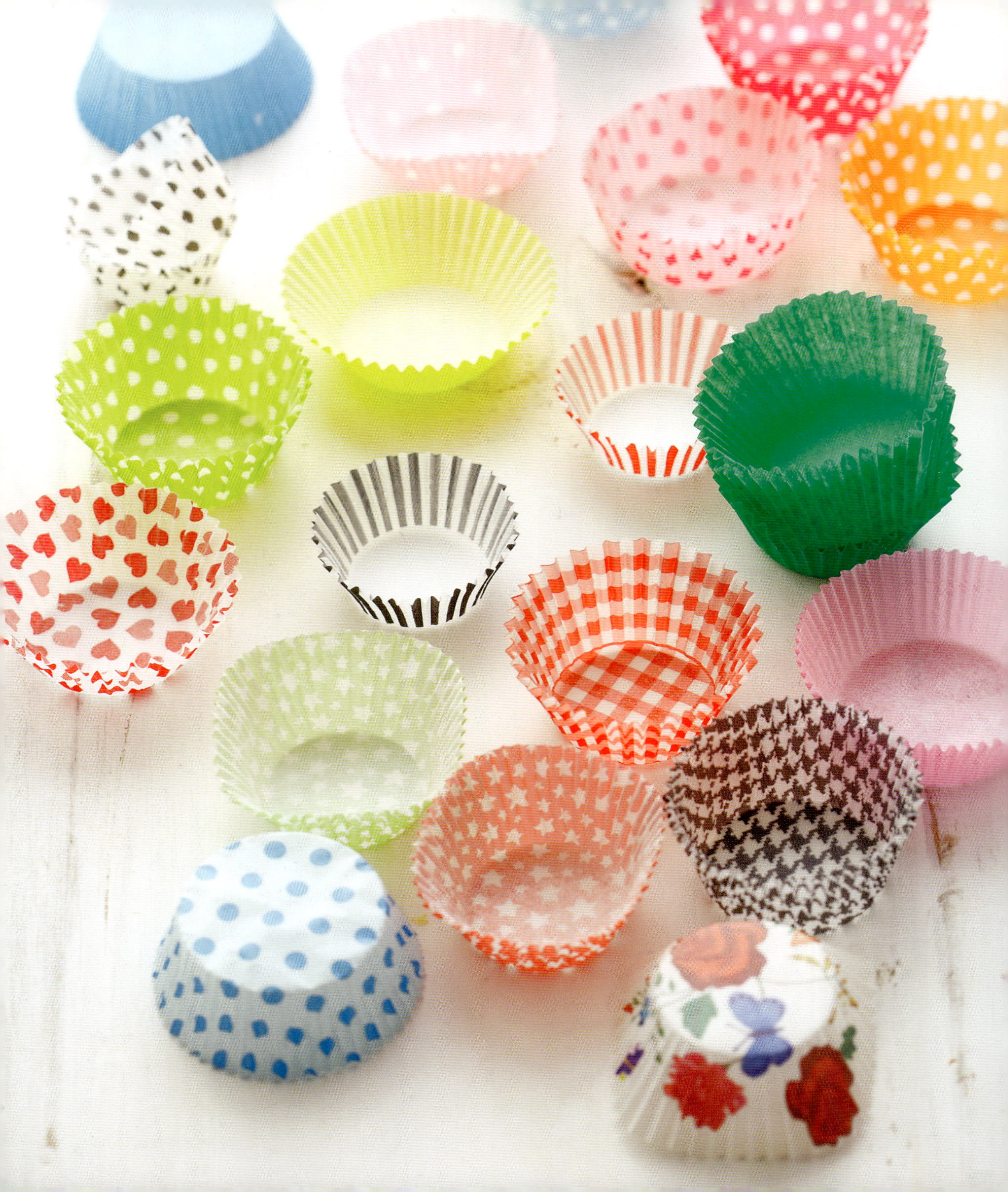

Index

A
all buttoned up 78
almond & apple cupcakes 18
apricot, sour cream & coconut cupcakes 8

B
baby bears 50
berries
   blueberry semolina cakes 29
   coconut & raspberry cupcakes 113
   low-fat berry cupcakes 22
   oatmeal & raspberry cupcakes 17
   peach & raspberry cupcakes 101
   pretty in pink 43
   raspberry balsamic cupcakes 92
blueberry semolina cakes 29
brownie cupcakes, triple chocolate 39
buttercreams 123
butterfly cakes 24

C
candied citrus zest 119
caramel buttercream 123
caramel and walnut cupcakes 95
cherry cupcakes 11

chocolate
   baby bears 50
   choc-hazelnut cupcakes 44
   chocolate buttercream 123
   chocolate butterfly cakes 24
   chocolate chip cupcakes 45
   chocolate cupcakes 116, 117
   chocolate fudge icing 39
   chocolate ganache 120
   chocolate glacé icing 121
   chocolate sauce 32
   flourless chocolate cakes 88
   marbled cupcakes 58
   orange white chocolate cupcakes 102
   pretty in pink 43
   rich dark chocolate cupcakes 108
   rocky road cupcakes 35
   triple chocolate brownie cupcakes 39
   your number's up 77
Christmas pudding cakes, mini 104
cinnamon & fig cupcakes 103
cinnamon sugar 49
citrus
   buttercreams 123
   candied citrus zest 119
   glacé icings 121
   intense mandarin cupcakes 110
   lemon cupcakes 116, 117
   lemon meringue cupcakes 91

   lime delicious cupcakes 107
   little marmalade cakes 15
   orange cupcakes 116, 117
   orange white chocolate cupcakes 102
   poppy seed cupcakes with orange syrup 24–5
coconut
   apricot, sour cream & coconut cupcakes 8
   coconut & raspberry cupcakes 113
   mini fluffy coconut cupcakes 16
cone cakes, lickable 46
cream cheese frosting 120
creatures
   baby bears 50
   funny faces 54
   hungry worms 62
   this little piggy 36
   zebra stripes 66
cupcake swirls 65
cupcakes
   flavours 117
   sizes 116

D
daisy cakes 85
dark chocolate ganache 120
dotty cakes 70

E
espresso cakes 97

F

flourless chocolate cakes 88
fluffy coconut cupcakes, mini 16
frostings *see* icings
fruit
   almond & apple cupcakes 18
   apricot, sour cream & coconut cupcakes 8
   cherry cupcakes 11
   cinnamon & fig cupcakes 103
   go bananas 57
   passionfruit cupcakes 26
   peach & raspberry cupcakes 101
   plum & cardamom cakes 94
   rhubarb, hazelnut & brown sugar crumble cakes 98
   sticky date cupcakes 109
   see also berries; citrus
funny faces 54

G

ganache, chocolate 120
gingerbread cupcakes 21
glacé icings 121
gluten-free cupcakes 118
go bananas 57

H

honey pot cupcakes 53
hungry worms 62

I

ice cream sundae cupcakes 32
icings
   choc-hazelnut 44
   chocolate fudge 39
   coffee 97
   cream cheese 120
   ginger 21
   glacé icings 121
   peanut butter cream 40
   royal icing 119
intense mandarin cupcakes 110

J

jam
   all buttoned up 78
   butterfly cakes 24
   jam doughnut cupcakes 49
   little marmalade cakes 15
   make it sparkle 82
   stampin' cupcakes 74
   stripe-a-luscious 81
jumping jelly beans 73

L

lamington cupcakes 12
lemon buttercream 123
lemon cupcakes 116, 117
lemon glacé icing 121
lemon meringue cupcakes 91
lickable cone cakes 46
lime buttercream 123
lime delicious cupcakes 107
lime glacé icing 121
little marmalade cakes 15
low-fat berry cupcakes 22

M

make it sparkle 82
marbled cupcakes 58
marshmallow
   daisy cakes 85
   rocky road cupcakes 35
   this little piggy 36
milk chocolate ganache 120
mini Christmas pudding cakes 104
mini fluffy coconut cupcakes 16

N

nuts
   almond & apple cupcakes 18
   caramel and walnut cupcakes 95
   choc-hazelnut cupcakes 44
   ice cream sundae cupcakes 32
   peanut butter cupcakes 40
   rhubarb, hazelnut & brown sugar crumble cakes 98
   rocky road cupcakes 35

O

oatmeal & raspberry cupcakes 17
orange buttercream 123
orange cupcakes 116, 117
orange glacé icing 121
orange syrup 25
orange white chocolate cupcakes 102

P

passionfruit cupcakes 26
peach & raspberry cupcakes 101
peanut butter cupcakes 40
plum & cardamom cakes 94
poppy seed cupcakes with orange syrup 24–5
pretty in pink 43

R

raspberry balsamic cupcakes 92
rhubarb, hazelnut & brown sugar crumble cakes 98
rich dark chocolate cupcakes 108
rocky road cupcakes 35
royal icing 119

S

semolina and blueberry cakes 29
stampin' cupcakes 74
sticky date cupcakes 109
stripes
   stripe-a-luscious 81
   zebra stripes 66
sweet hearts 69

T

this little piggy 36
toppings *see* icings
triple chocolate brownie cupcakes 39

V

vanilla buttercream 123
vanilla cupcakes 116

W

white chocolate ganache 120
writing fudge 62

Y

your number's up 77

Z

zebra stripes 66
zest, candied citrus 119

Published in 2012 by Murdoch Books Pty Limited

Murdoch Books Australia
Pier 8/9
23 Hickson Road
Millers Point NSW 2000
Phone: +61 (0) 2 8220 2000
Fax: +61 (0) 2 8220 2558
www.murdochbooks.com.au

Murdoch Books UK Limited
Erico House, 6th Floor
93–99 Upper Richmond Road
Putney, London SW15 2TG
Phone: +44 (0) 20 8785 5995
Fax: +44 (0) 20 8785 5985
www.murdochbooks.co.uk

Publisher: Anneka Manning
Project Editor: Alice Grundy
Copy Editor: Melissa Penn
Food Editor: Grace Campbell
Design concept: Alex Frampton and Vivien Valk
Design layout: R.T.J. Klinkhamer
Photographer: Michele Aboud
Stylist: Sarah de Nardi
Illustrator: Alex Frampton
Production Controller: Joan Beal

Recipe development: Sonia Greig, Leanne Kitchen, Kirrily La Rosa, Kim Meredith, Kathy Knudsen
Food preparation for photography: Grace Campbell

Text copyright © Murdoch Books Pty Limited 2012
Design and photography copyright © Murdoch Books Pty Limited 2012

All rights reserved. No part of this publication may be reproduced, stored in a retrieval system or transmitted in any form or by any means, electronic, mechanical, photocopying, recording or otherwise, without the prior written permission of the publisher.

National Library of Australia Cataloguing-in-Publication Data

Title:	Make Me Cupcakes
ISBN:	978-1-74266-323-4 (pbk.)
Series:	Make me.
Notes:	Includes index.
Subjects:	Cupcakes, Cake decorating.
Dewey Number:	641.8653

A catalogue record for this book is available from the British Library.

Printed by 1010 Printing International Limited, China

CONVERSION GUIDE: Cooking times may vary depending on the oven you are using. For fan-forced ovens, as a general rule, set the oven temperature to 20°C (35°F) lower than indicated in the recipe. We have used 20 ml (4 teaspoon) tablespoon measures. If you are using a 15 ml (3 teaspoon) tablespoon, add an extra teaspoon for each tablespoon specified. We have used 60 g (Grade 3) eggs in all recipes.